COMING OUT WHILE STAYING IN

COMING OUT WHILE STAYING IN

LEANNE MCCALL TIGERT

STRUGGLES AND CELEBRATIONS OF LESBIANS, GAYS, AND BISEXUALS IN THE CHURCH

United Church Press
Cleveland, Ohio

United Church Press, Cleveland, Ohio 44115
© 1996 by Leanne McCall Tigert

Biblical quotations are from the New Revised Standard Version of
the Bible, © 1989 by the Division of Christian Education of the
National Council of the Churches of Christ in the U.S.A., and are
used by permission

Printed in the United States of America on acid-free paper

01   00   99   98   97   96   5   4   3   2   1

Library of Congress Cataloging-in-Publication Data

Tigert, Leanne McCall, 1957–
      Coming out while staying in : struggles and celebrations of
   lesbians, gays, and bisexuals in the church / Leanne McCall
   Tigert.
          p.   cm.
      Includes bibliographical references (p.   ).
      ISBN 0-8298-1150-8 (alk. paper)
      1. Homosexuality—Religious aspects—Christianity.
   2. Church work with gays.   3. United Church of Christ—Membership.   4. United Church of Christ—Doctrines.   I. Title.
   BR115.H6T54   1996
   261.8'35766—dc20   96-28737
                                                             CIP

This book is written in honor of the numerous lesbian, gay, and bisexual persons who have given and will continue to give of their very selves and souls to liberate the church from the bondage of fear and shame. For those who have gone before me, I feel great respect and awe at the barriers you have broken in order for the rest of us to walk through. For those who walk with me, I feel great affection and warmth, for you have indeed become my brothers and my sisters, as together we seek the will of God. For those who will come after me, I am hopeful and smile with wonder at the places you and God may take us all.

Contents

Acknowledgments ix

Introduction: The Significance of "Coming Out" While "Staying In": A Personal Journey of Spirituality and Sexuality xiii

1 Family Secrets: Gay/Lesbian/Bisexuality; Homophobia and Heterosexism in the Church 1

2 Where We Are, Where We Have Been, Where We Are Going: A Brief Overview of the Gay/Lesbian/Bisexual Movement in Mainline Churches 29

3 The Body of Christ: Functional or Dysfunctional System? 47

4 A Liberating Theology of the Church 79

5 The Journey toward Sexual and Spiritual Liberation 96

6 Stories of Hurting, Stories of Healing: Lesbian, Gay, and Bisexual Persons Speak of Their Experiences in the Church 115

7 Conclusions, Implications, and Suggestions for Ministry 131

Appendix A: Interview Questionnaire 149

Appendix B: Welcoming Congregation Statements from Several Denominations; UCC Pronouncements and Resolutions regarding Lesbian/Gay/Bisexual Concerns 151

Appendix C: Christian Organizations Focusing on Lesbian and Gay Concerns in the United States 163

Notes 169

Bibliography 175

Acknowledgments

The older I get, the more I have come to realize that the "acknowledgments" can often be the most interesting part of a book. Perhaps I have come to know the truth in the saying, "It takes a whole village to raise a child." Likewise, it takes a whole community—in fact, a convergence of communities—to write a book. As I read other books written by sisters and brothers seeking liberation, I find that I recognize people, places, and events that have become a part of their work. Indeed, the work, the people, and the events overlap and come together to form a picture that is far greater, larger, and deeper than any one of us alone. I know that I could not have begun to write this in isolation, anymore than I could have lived it in isolation.

I want to begin by thanking the women and men who are unnamed in this book but in fact are its very heart and soul. It has been an honor to sit with people in formal interviews and informal conversations as they have shared themselves so honestly and candidly with me. I hope that my efforts can do justice to the integrity and depth of spirit that is within each of them.

This book began as my project for the Doctor of Ministry degree in pastoral psychology at Andover Newton Theological School. I want to thank Dr. Brita Gill-Austern, my project adviser, for her help, support, and challenge at that time. I would never have stretched this far had she not encouraged and pushed me. Also, I thank Rev. Dr. Phillip Joseph Mayher, whose encouragement and advice enabled me to seek publication, and Margaret Landsman for proofreading the manuscript.

I also wish to thank those at United Church Press for their support and assistance through the process. Between Kim Sadler's gracious spirit, Kelley Baker's willingness to respond quickly and professionally, and everyone's help, I was able to move through the difficulties of publishing my first book.

I wish to thank the members of Spirit of the Mountains, a gay/straight justice-seeking congregation, for being who you are, when and where you are. It is an honor to be pastor to persons seeking new models of being "church" together, in difficult times and places. Also, I offer my heartfelt gratitude to the members of the United Church Coalition for Lesbian/Gay Concerns (UCCL/GC). Together you form a powerful base community for many of us. I am especially grateful to the Coalition Choir, enabling me to sing my spirit in a way that has not yet been possible anywhere else, to the national coordinators and council who work diligently in the care and maintenance of this community. I also wish to thank the Rev. Ann B. Day, coordinator of the ONA program, for her dedication, wisdom, and encouragement through this time, along with various Welcoming Church coordinators for their information and encouragement.

It is often very difficult to live in a place as politically and socially conservative as New Hampshire (although the mountains are beautiful). Building community dedicated to justice, as encouraged by the leaders of the New Hampshire Conference of the United Church of Christ, has been significant in my own ability to remain here. I am grateful to those persons who continue to keep the conference ONA resolution alive, despite the powerful social and political forces that would bury it if they could. I wish to thank the Rev. Carole Carlson, New Hampshire Conference minister, for her personal and professional support. She read (and reread) my manuscript and has been a confidant, pastor, and friend throughout numerous vocational and personal struggles and changes.

I also wish to thank my colleagues at Womankind Counseling Center in Concord, New Hampshire. They were patient and supportive through the process, especially when my mind was preoccupied with writing. They are a wonderful group of feminist psychotherapists/advocates, with whom I feel grateful to work.

On a more personal note, I wish to thank my parents, who instilled in me at a very young age the sacredness of church community which has carried me through to this day. I am also grateful to my friends, Joyce, Sheila, Marianne, Lisa, Amy, and others, who have patiently (for the most part) temporarily given up a hiking, blading, and coffee-drinking "buddy" while I have spent too much time at the computer. It's time to play!

I need to acknowledge my dog, Abbie, who lived with me for nine years and was then shot and killed during a time when I was being harassed. Her memory continues to haunt me, as she has been present during the writing of this book. We now have a new dog, Amos, who jumps every time I get up from the computer, in hopes that it is time for the much-anticipated walk.

I wish to acknowledge my beautiful stepchildren, Rachel and Sarah, who continue to remind me that telling jokes and giggling around the dinner table are as sacred as working, praying, or writing for justice. Finally, I want to express my awe, my gratitude, my deep affection and love for my partner, soulmate, and friend, Emily Geoghegan. It is my living and loving with her that make the rest of my life more meaningful.

Introduction:

The Significance of "Coming Out" While "Staying In": A Personal Journey of Spirituality and Sexuality

This book has been years in the making, not so much in the writing as in the doing and living. Essentially, I have been making the conscious journey of sexuality and spirituality since I was twenty years old. During that year I "came out" as a lesbian to myself and to the pastor of the church in which I served as youth minister. Although the congregation had expressed great satisfaction with my work, the pastor fired me immediately upon learning of my sexual orientation. I did not argue; I did not take a stand; I did not call anyone else to share my pain or strategize my response. I simply cleaned out my office, turned in my key, and walked quietly out of the door. As I made my way to the car I thought, "Maybe he's right. I know that I'm good at my work in the church. I know that it's the only work I can imagine myself doing, I know the church is my home and I can't imagine being without it, but maybe all that gets wiped out and doesn't matter if I admit who I really am. Maybe God doesn't have a place for the real me."

Since that time I have been led and have traveled a long way on a very demanding, often scary, as well as powerfully healing journey of faith. I now know God's creative and liberating love for me as a lesbian. I celebrate the life I have found with my partner, our children, my friends and the family members who have grown in their own understanding and acceptance of diversity (and those who continue to challenge me in my own growth process). I celebrate the steps I have taken out of the closet, the healing and health these steps have brought me, and the spiritual community I have found within and outside of the church.

I also know the painful reality that God's liberating love and the church's institutionalization of that love can be radically different. I was ordained as a minister in the United Church of Christ twelve years ago. At that time, conversations about homosexuality and religion were not common on a local church level; nor was I ready emotionally, spiritually, or psychologically to risk being "out," and so I remained closeted. The prevailing practice in the church then often mirrored the present-day military policy of "Don't ask, don't tell." Many members of the congregation and of the Committee on Ministry were aware of my sexual orientation; however, it was as if we had all conspired not to talk about it. I certainly held my breath, hoping that no one would raise the issue and at the same time wishing the silence would end. I knew that to come out probably would mean the end of my hopes for ordination in that time and place, even though I was again being told that my work as youth minister was adding new life not only to the local church but to the association as well. Being fired was a scene I did not want to repeat. I also knew (as I still know) that I was called to ordained parish ministry, and I wanted at least the chance to pursue that call.

Since that time, I have served two local churches and am currently serving as pastor of Spirit of the Mountains, a worshiping community whose primary mission is to reach out to the lesbian, gay, and bisexual community and their friends and families in New Hampshire. I also work as a certified pastoral counselor in a not-for-profit feminist counseling center and am a fellow in the American Association of Pastoral Counselors.

As a pastor and a counselor, I have listened to the life stories of many gay, lesbian, and bisexual persons seeking to affirm themselves and to be part of a faith community. However, the experience of so much rejection and oppression has led many to the conclusion that it is unhealthy at least, and impossible at most, to be part of a mainline congregation and yet be a self-affirming, healthy gay/lesbian/bisexual person. This rejection and oppression have been manifest in a variety of ways: verbal, physical, and sexual harassment; negative body language; the omission of images, symbols, and concerns relevant to lesbian, gay, and bisexual persons; attempts at "conversion" to heterosexuality; denial/disbelief of one's sexual orientation; and silence.

Rejection and oppression have also emerged from within rather than from outside the self, with an internalization of self-denigrating and condemning attitudes. This internalized homophobia often prevents a person from feeling loved and worthy of spiritual communion as one of God's children.

As an active member of the lesbian/gay/bisexual political and social community, I have listened to lesbian/gay/bisexual persons ask me, "Why bother with the Christian church? What's the point? With its history of discrimination and oppression, how can it possibly benefit us?"

At the same time, I have heard repeatedly three statements from many heterosexual persons in the church. First, some have said, "Our history proclaims our openness: Our church sign says, 'All Welcome,' so why should we do something extra for this population in particular?" Second, some have said, "Open to gay people? Sure, anyone can come here. But don't make me be affirming." (This can be translated as, "I'll tolerate them, but I don't believe and won't act as if they are equal to me.") Then they ask, "So why aren't they here?" Finally, others have said, "We want to do more. We want to be an inclusive body of Christ, but what can we do?" These questions are not rhetorical; they are concrete, and they come out of the real experiences of real people of faith.

Through my own experiences in the church, I have developed a "love/hate" relationship with it. I have known the most healing, hope-filled, spiritually connected, profound moments of my life within the community of faith, the body of Christ. I have also known the most painful, alienating, demoralizing, scary, and sad moments of my life within the institution of the church. These are experiences of extremes—of deep love and hate. Perhaps these conflicting feelings are shared by many for a variety of reasons, and are best interpreted as the power and pitfalls of the organization, or the mediation of salvation and sin within a human-divine community.

In the spring of 1989, I "came out" to my local congregation and to the annual meeting of the New Hampshire Conference, in which I was serving as a local church pastor. On that day, an old familiar hymn I grew up with kept playing in my head. On the following Sunday morning, as I was sitting in my study preparing for worship, I heard the choir begin to sing the very same hymn:

> Lead me Lord, lead me in thy righteousness,
> Make thy way plain before my face.
> For it is thou, Lord, thou Lord only,
> That makest me dwell in safety.[1]

I knew when I heard this hymn that I was indeed being led in the way of righteousness to claim publicly who I am within the community of the United Church of Christ. I also knew, as I know even more surely now, that the only true safety for anyone is in the arms of God. However, this is especially true for those of us who live as the objects of homophobic hatred and violence.

I believe that the UCC is experiencing a journey of spirituality and sexuality that is powerful, exciting, frightening, sometimes hopeful, sometimes disappointing, and also sacred. During the past several years, the concerns of lesbian, gay, and bisexual persons within the United Church of Christ have "come out of the closet" on many levels. The process began with the "Resolution on Homosexuals and the Law," adopted by the Council for Christian Social Action on April 12, 1969; it continued in the General Synod Open and Affirming resolution in 1985; and it flourishes today in conference, association, and local church study processes, and in nondiscrimination and "Open and Affirming votes" (see appendix B). Through these steps in the coming-out process, the concerns of lesbian, gay, and bisexual persons have come into many people's conscious minds, and significant progress has been made.

Two recent examples of the power of gay/lesbian/bisexual concerns to speak for and to many occurred in June 1995 at the national gathering of United Church Coalition for Lesbian/Gay

Concerns (UCCL/GC) in Berkeley, California. During the first evening's celebration of worship, Dr. Paul Sherry, the president of the United Church of Christ, spoke to those gathered, saying, "It is this Coalition for Lesbian/Gay Concerns that is leading the United Church of Christ into a revival." Obviously, we are not just on our own self-interested and self-focused trip, but are engaged in the work of bringing about God's Shalom with all.

A few days later during the meeting of General Synod (the bi-annual national meeting of the denomination), the UCCL/GC Coalition Choir sang at a morning worship service. In this service, we were introducing music from *The New Century Hymnal*. At the conclusion of this service, we were offered the opportunity to sing a choral hymn of our choice. Thus, we chose one that we had learned from our choir director, the Rev. Rick Yramategui, "We Shall Not Be Silent":

> We shall not be silent, nor shall the earth remain unmoved …
> And if our voice were broken, still the stones themselves
> would cry …
> Should every voice be stilled, and ancient dreams be killed;
> Should all our hoping die, the stones themselves would cry;
> On earth is not God's equal.[2]

While singing, I looked across the sea of faces of the hundreds of delegates and noticed that many were crying. At the end, we received a long, standing ovation from virtually the entire body. I knew then that Paul Sherry was right. Through song, prayer, struggle, and celebration, we are leading the entire church to a revival and revolution of justice and love. What was once for many just an "issue" has become a kind of Kairos moment of struggle for the liberation of real people with real lives of pain and hope.

Out of all these experiences, individual and institutional, this book emerges. My hope in writing is to express some of the *realness* of the journey toward liberation for lesbian/gay/bisexual people within the United Church of Christ. As you will learn in chapter 2, this journey certainly is not limited to the

UCC; there are movements like it in all major denominations. In fact, there is an ecumenical groundswell of the cry and work for justice and liberation for lesbian/gay/bisexual persons throughout mainline Protestant churches. This is most notably seen in the "Welcoming Congregations" movement (an interdenominational movement encouraging local congregations to declare themselves welcoming of gay/lesbian/bisexual persons, which will be explored further in chapter 2). Nonetheless, it is the United Church of Christ with which I am the most familiar; it is my spiritual home, although I was raised in the United Methodist tradition. I hope that all readers from the UCC and other denominations will benefit from reading this, along with lesbian/gay/bisexual persons seeking to find a spiritual home.

The Scope and Purpose of This Book

My purpose in writing this book is to provide the reader with a keen understanding of the power and impact of homophobia, and the experience of oppression of lesbian, gay, and bisexual persons within the church. In doing so, I hope to present possibilities for change, healing, and liberation that can touch the lives of all, including heterosexual persons.

I will discuss the experience of oppression and the possibilities for liberation through the dual perspectives of psychology and theology. The underlying assumption here is that the interweaving of these two disciplines is formative in the experience of both sexuality and spirituality. Therefore, I will offer a *theology* of liberation that leads to and is interwoven with a *psychology* of liberation for lesbian, gay, and bisexual persons, and an ecclesiastical understanding of the church which empowers it for the ministry of liberation. Finally, I hope to offer some suggestions for ministry for those who are seeking to take further steps in their parish or community in this journey of sexuality and spirituality.

In order to accomplish this purpose, I will explain family systems and object-relations theories as they apply to the church—topics essential to an understanding of how we structure ourselves psychologically and socially and the ensuing effects on lesbian/gay/bisexual persons. Unless we are mindful of the psychosocial and theological roles we have played, we will be stuck in the futile exercise (or perhaps the defense) of giving mere lip service to justice—making pronouncements, writing studies, participating in discussions, without making any real structural changes. I will combine this psychological approach with a theological one—that of liberation theology, along with my own research and experience.

Chapter 1, "Family Secrets: Homophobia and Heterosexism in the Church," identifies and explains homophobia and heterosexism as forms of discrimination, focusing on the functions and manifestations of these forces within the church and society, and their psychological impact on gay/lesbian/bisexual persons, as well as on Christian congregations.

Chapter 2, "Where We Have Been, Where We Are, Where We Hope to Go," provides a brief overview of the "Welcoming Congregations" and the justice/advocacy movement across several denominations. Although this can in no way describe fully the experience in every communion, it may capture the flavor of the movement toward justice and the place of sexual minorities across denominations.

Chapter 3, "The Body of Christ: Functional or Dysfunctional System?" presents some of the core concepts of family-systems theory. I believe this is particularly pertinent to and helpful in addressing such concepts as roles and relationships, positions and power, and change within a system such as the church. Salvador Minuchin asserts that modifying the structure of the family itself can become the vehicle for healing which enables it to carry out the family's valued tasks.[3] This assertion is easily applied to the system of the church. In other words, the church is organized around sacramental, prophetic, nurturing, justice-making, and other functions. However, the relational structure of the institution often prevents it from performing these functions in regard to the lives of lesbian/gay/bisexual persons. According to Minuchin's theory, healing occurs in the re-working of these structures so that the church can be about what it is called to be and do. It is hoped that these theories in particular can help to demystify the structure of interactions, patterns, images, beliefs, and assumptions that support homophobia and heterosexism within the church, thereby opening up possibilities for change.

Chapter 4, "The Body of Christ: A Liberating Theology of the Church," sets forth a theological understanding of the church as the people called out of injustice into liberation. This understanding incorporates the biblical story of the Israelites called out of slavery as the foundation to our worship and community life. I will combine this with descriptive images from the gospels and epistles which name the church as the inclusive and just embodiment of Christ. This is critical to the formation of a liberating community.

Chapter 5, "The Journey toward Sexual and Spiritual Liberation," builds on the foundation laid in previous chapters, offering a theology of liberation for gay/lesbian/bisexual persons within the framework of the Christian faith and church. This liberation theology will provide constructs, images, and assertions which emerge out of the praxis (a model of action and reflection) of gay/lesbian/bisexual persons' experience of the church and spiritual/sexual community. This is intended to invite the reader into a dialogue between his or her own action and reflection.

Chapter 6, "Stories of Hurting, Stories of Healing: Gay/Lesbian/Bisexual Persons Speak of their Experiences in the Church," presents the results of a survey concerning the experience of homophobia and heterosexism in the UCC These results come from fifteen in-depth interviews I conducted over several months during 1993. I hope that this chapter will give the reader a sense of the real-life experiences and feelings of those who have struggled to be in relationship with the church.

The final chapter, "What Now," concludes with a focus on concrete suggestions and implications for ministry within various settings of the United Church of Christ (and as they relate to other denominations). I also include a section for gay/lesbian/bisexual persons who are seeking to find a spiritual home and sustenance within the church. These conclusions are informed by the psychological and theological foundations of this ministry and by the experience of being gay/lesbian/bisexual in the church.

You will notice a set of discussion questions at the end of each chapter. I hope that you will use these both individually and in small groups. They are intended to start you thinking theologically, psychologically, and faithfully about your own experience of gay, lesbian, and bisexual persons in the church. I hope these questions are only the beginning: In the spirit of the poet Rainer Marie Wilke, let us continue to ask the questions so that someday we will "live into the answers."

Assumptions

One always approaches any topic with certain assumptions in mind. Countless theological proclamations about homosexuality and the church have been made over time, each with its own set of implicit and explicit assumptions. Therefore, I want to be very clear about the starting point in my writing, and the theological and psychological beliefs that support it.

First, sexuality is a gift of the loving, passionate, Creator God. Included within this gift lies the diversity of sexual expression. Sexual orientation—lesbian, gay, heterosexual, or bisexual—is neither intrinsically good nor evil. Rather than judge people by their sexual orientation and its genital expression, persons should be held accountable to the ethics of love. This is expressed clearly by Norman Pittenger and James Nelson:

> Thus, the ethical question . . . is this: what sexual behavior will serve and enhance, rather than inhibit, damage, or destroy the fuller realization of our divinely-intended humanity? The answer is sexual behavior in accord with an ethics of love. This means commitment and trust, tenderness, respect, for the other, and the desire for ongoing and responsible communion with the other . . . an ethics of love mandates against selfish sexual expression, cruelty, impersonal sex, obsession with sex, and against actions done without willingness to take responsibility for the consequences. Such an ethics always asks about the meanings of acts in their total context—in the relationship itself, in society, and in regard to

God's intended direction for human life. Such an ethics of sexual love is equally appropriate to heterosexual and gay Christians. There is no double standard.[4]

Second, many individual Christians and faith communities are unclear about their belief stance toward homosexuality. In some instances, this may be the result of poor and/or rigid biblical interpretive skills, combined with a deafening silence in regard to a theology of sexuality and homosexuality. My experience thus far has convinced me that most people are less certain about their views and feelings on this subject than many church leaders assume. Often people express their belief that the Bible condemns homosexuality, although they are not exactly sure how or why. Few church members have been taught, or have arrived at their own, congruent theological stance toward sexuality and homosexuality .

Third, the Bible does not make a clear statement of judgment in regard to sexual orientation. The few references in scripture often misinterpreted to condemn homosexuality actually address issues of rape, lust, temple prostitution, the importance of procreation, and the sexist ideation that men and women are not to be treated equally. The Bible does not address sexual orientation as we know and understand it today.

Fourth, the Christian church has a contradictory history in regard to its treatment of lesbian/gay/bisexual persons. Sometimes this history has included ostracism and condemnation, while at other times it has incorporated the blessing of same-gender sexual and spiritual commitments. According to the work of John Boswell, early Christianity was not antigay and, in fact, supported same-gender commitments. However, as the surrounding culture and government became more hostile to eroticism and sexuality, so did the Christian tradition. Throughout modern history, the majority of the church's actions have condemned nonheterosexual persons, calling them sinners before God.

Not only does there appear to have been no general prejudice against gay people among early Christians; there does not seem to have been any reason for Christianity to adopt a hostile attitude toward homosexual behavior. Many prominent and respected Christians—some canonized—were involved in relationships which would almost certainly be considered homosexual. . . . Antierotic pressure from government and more ascetic schools of sexual ethics was in time (able) to induce a violently hostile reaction from Christianity itself.[5]

Fifth, the power of homophobia, in its spiritual, social, psychological, theological and ethical manifestations, is critical to comprehend in order to understand the lives of lesbian/gay/bisexual persons. Homophobia and heterosexism will be defined clearly in chapter 1; however, at this point it is important to state how these words are being used. The term *homophobia* was first coined by Dr. George Weinberg in 1972 and is defined as the fear of homosexuals and homosexuality.[6] Heterosexism is the system of belief in which heterosexuality is presumed to be the only acceptable life option.[7] In order to know the pain, fears, and needs—as well as the gifts and graces—of gay, lesbian, and bisexual Christians seeking spiritual communion, one must know about the experience and power of homophobia and heterosexism and their psychological, social, and spiritual effects on individuals.

Sixth, the body of Christ cannot be well as long as one member suffers. Thus, to honor the hurt and to seek healing of one part of the body brings honor and healing to the whole. "If one member suffers, all suffer together with it; if one member is honored, all rejoice together with it" (1 Cor. 12:26).

Seventh, the good news of the Christian faith is truly a gospel of liberation. The experience of homophobia within the church stands in total contradiction of "the freedom of new life in Christ." The liberation movement of lesbian, gay, and bisexual persons is both different from and similar to other movements for justice throughout the church universal.

Eighth, psychological health and well-being are greatly affected by the integration of a person's sexuality and sexual orientation, as well as his/her ability to be "out." In other words, the keeping of secrets, whether to protect one's job, one's professional standing, one's family, or one's safety, is harmful to oneself.

The internalization of homophobic attitudes creates significant psychological and spiritual harm, not only for gay, lesbian, and bisexual person, but for heterosexual persons as well.

Ninth, by maintaining a system in which lesbian/gay/bisexual persons feel that they must either remain closeted or leave altogether, the church is losing a tremendous resource of leadership, vision, and creativity.

Tenth, the United Church of Christ has done as much as or more than any other Protestant faith communion in addressing the issue of homosexuality. Inquiring into the work of this denomination—one that affirms both unity and diversity as critical to identity and theology—has meaning and ramifications for all faith communities. According to the work of Christopher Carrington, as referred to in chapter 6, this may be the result of the combination of structure and values. At the present, there are numerous individuals and congregations throughout the church expressing their desire for help in understanding the experiences and needs of nonheterosexual persons seeking faith community. Many will welcome any work, with specific examples and suggestions, that addresses this area of inquiry.

Obviously, a book such as this raises many questions that cannot be answered within the body of this writing. For example, I am not directly discussing the biblical references to homosexuality or presenting a systematic theology of sexuality. Therefore, I would like to refer the reader to other resources for further inquiry. For biblical interpretation, I suggest *Is the Homosexual My Neighbor? A Positive Christian Response,* Revised and Updated, by Virginia Ramey Mollencott and Letha Scanzoni; *What the Bible Really Says about Homosexuality,* by Daniel Helminiak; and *The Word Is Out: The Bible Reclaimed for Lesbians and Gay Men—365 Daily Meditations,* by Chris Glaser. Each of these writings presents easily accessible, solid scriptural exegesis regarding sexual orientation. I believe that James B. Nelson's *Embodiment: An Approach to Sexuality and Christian Theology* should be required reading for any Christian seeking a faithful and holistic approach to sexuality. I also recommend *Sexuality and the Sacred,* by James B. Nelson and Sandra P. Longfellow. In the area of church history as regards homosexuality, I recommend John Boswell's scholarly, in-depth research in *Christianity, Homosexuality, and Social Tolerance.*

Finally, I am encouraged by the work being done and the voices being raised throughout the church concerning this particular issue. I trust that together God is leading us into a time of true Shalom in which we will all "dwell in safety."

Questions for Discussion

1. What are your hopes and fears as you begin reading and/or discussing this book?

2. Are you conscious of your own journey in relating sexuality and spirituality? Can you describe significant milestones in this journey (memories, images, etc.)?

3. When did you first hear about homosexuality or become aware of gay, lesbian, and bisexual people? When did you first encounter this issue in the church?

4. If you are gay, lesbian, or bisexual, how has your own church experience alienated or welcomed you? If you are heterosexual, how has your church welcomed or alienated gay, lesbian, and bisexual persons?

5. What are your assumptions/beliefs about sexuality, sexual orientation, scripture, and homophobia?

6. Do you believe that the church needs to address the issues of homophobia and heterosexism? Why or why not?

Family Secrets: Gay/Lesbian/Bisexuality; Homophobia and Heterosexism in the Church

Gay/Lesbian/Bisexuality

When addressing the issues of gay/lesbian/bisexual persons within the church, I have come across numerous situations in which people have had enormous difficulty communicating with one another. This difficulty has often been the result of heated emotions and radically different belief systems, as well as differing interpretations of terms.

For example, in one Open and Affirming study session in which I was participating, it became clear that someone did not know that *lesbian* referred to women and not to men. At another time, a study participant stated that he believed that there were numerous versions of "bisexuality," including bestiality. The terms *homosexual, gay, lesbian,* and *bisexual* often connote different meanings to different individuals, depending on their experience, history, and knowledge. Therefore, I wish to offer brief definitions and descriptions of how they are used in this book. For further information and appropriate definitions regarding sexual orientation, I suggest reading *Looking at Gay and Lesbian Life,* by Warren J. Blumenfeld and Diane Raymond,[1] especially chapter 1, "Socialization and Gender Roles"; *Gay American History: Lesbians and Gay Men in the U.S.A.,*[2] by Jonathan Katz; and *Psychological Perspectives on Lesbian and Gay Male Experiences,* edited by Linda D. Garnets and Douglas C. Kimmel.[3]

Perhaps the most significant differences between the terms *homosexual* and *gay/lesbian* are descriptive ones. Each term describes same-sex attraction; however, *homosexual* historically has had negative connotations related only to behavior (as defined by heterosexuals), and has often left women invisible. On

the other hand, the terms *gay* and *lesbian* express a more affirming sense of self-identity and connection to a larger community. Same-sex sexual behavior has been in existence as long
as humans have existed; however, categories of sexual orientation are a nineteenth- and twentieth-century invention. During
the last two hundred years, same-gender sexual orientation has
come to tell something of one's personal identity rather than
simply one's sexual behavior. This is, in large part, due to the
work of the homophile rights and feminist movements for justice. (The first-known gay rights organization began in Germany in the late 1800s.)

Many people think of the modern gay/lesbian liberation
movement as having had its birth in the Stonewall riot of 1969.
On June 28 of that year, the police raided the Stonewall Inn in
the Greenwich Village area of New York City. Although police
had often raided gay bars in the past, on this particular night, the
bar patrons fought back, demanding their civil and human
rights. A sense of community empowerment and activism was
crystallized in this event, and Stonewall continues to be a compelling symbol of the work of gay/lesbian liberation.

Today, across the country during the month of June, members and supporters of the gay/lesbian/bisexual/transgendered
community gather for the annual pride march and coinciding
events. In small towns like Concord, New Hampshire, several
hundred persons may gather on the capitol steps, while in large
cities like New York and San Francisco, more than one hundred
thousand people come together to celebrate gay pride. According to Irvashi Vaid, a prominent leader in the gay/lesbian movement, gay/lesbian liberation changed the face of its predecessor,
the homophile movement, in significant ways.

> The gay and lesbian liberation movement introduced four ideas
> into the existing homophile movement: (1) the notion that com-
> ing out and pursuing gay and lesbian visibility held the key to our
> freedom; (2) that queer freedom would profoundly change gen-
> der roles, sexism, and heterosexual institutions like the family;
> (3) that gay, lesbian, and bisexual people were an integral part of
> the broad demand for social change and needed a political phi-

losophy that made connections to race, gender, and economic issues; and (4) that the creation of a gay and lesbian counterculture
was an essential part of establishing lesbian and gay identity.[4]

In contrast, the term *homosexual* has been used primarily as
a description of sexual behavior and, due to its history, often car-
ries negative connotations for gay and lesbian people. For example, the American Psychological Association Committee on
Lesbian and Gay concerns wrote: "The word *homosexual* has several problems of designation. First, it may perpetuate negative
stereotypes because of its historical associations with pathology
and criminal behavior. Second, it is ambiguous in reference because it is often assumed to refer exclusively to men and thus
renders lesbians invisible. Third, it is often unclear."[5] Therefore,
it is important to be clear in our language as to whether we are
describing genital sexual behavior or a self-identified sexual,
emotional, and social identity.

Another term that has recently come to the forefront of people's consciousness is *bisexual*. This is an often misunderstood
and misappropriated label. Like *homosexual,* the word *bisexual*
describes a certain object-choice, or affectional-sexual orienta-
tion/attraction. Most research concludes that sexual orientation
needs to be understood as a continuum, with each of us falling
at different points, some more homosexual and others more
heterosexual (see the Kinsey reports of 1948 and 1953). Sigmund Freud suggested that all humans are born with bisexual
potential, and that for unknown reasons (socialization, biology),
we become either predominantly heterosexual or predominantly homosexual.

Although research is still limited, there is some evidence
suggesting that bisexuals go though a different developmental
process than either heterosexuals or homosexuals.

Until recently no one has developed a model for bisexual identity. . . . [T]he major differences . . . as compared to homosexuals
were that bisexuals had earlier heterosexual experiences, added
their homosexual identity to an already formed heterosexual
identity. . . . [R]esults also countered the myth that bisexuals are

equally attracted to both genders . . . (they rarely exhibited equal attractions, feelings, or behaviors toward both sexes . . .). [I]f the bisexual was in a relationship with a same-sex partner he or she identified as gay or lesbian, if the partner was of the other gender then the identification was as a heterosexual.[6]

With this observation in mind, persons who call themselves bisexual are often misunderstood and looked down on by gays, lesbians, and heterosexuals alike. I know that in my own pastoral and personal experience, I have come to learn that naming oneself as bisexual may in fact be a step in the process of coming out as gay or lesbian. Perhaps this identification feels less threatening within a prejudiced and oppressive society; perhaps it is a normal and necessary step in the process of moving from one place on the continuum to another. Nevertheless, it is a gross misjudgment to believe that naming oneself as bisexual is always such an interim step. The emergence of a self-identified bisexual community demanding a place in the movement for gay and lesbian liberation is a relatively new phenomenon which deserves its rightful place in the journey to liberation.

There are others who are beginning to "come out of the closet," telling their stories and seeking to be included in the struggle for liberation. Specifically, these are persons in the transgendered community, which includes transsexuals, transvestites, and cross-dressers. Again, these persons go through a very different developmental process from gay/lesbian persons, raise different issues and concerns about gender identity, and face enormous prejudice and suffering. Although in this book I do not deal directly with the concerns of transgendered persons, I applaud their courage and witness in telling their stories, and I trust that the church will continue to be challenged and grow in its understanding of sexuality and gender.

Homophobia and Heterosexism

Another area of much disagreement in meaning is in regard to the words, "homophobia" and "heterosexism." Like any word trying to describe a human attitude, these words are often believed to be subjective and open to personal interpretation. In one church discussion group, I witnessed one person making an antigay/lesbian/bisexual statement ("They can worship here, but they can't have any kind of union service here"). This statement was followed by someone else naming this assertion as "homophobic." This was in turn followed by, "You're being phobic about my beliefs because they are different from yours." Obviously, this discussion did not get very far.

In this book, I wish to define and place into context the words *homophobia* and *heterosexism*. I believe the reader will find that their interpretation is neither as subjective nor as personal as some might suggest.

Homophobia

Homophobia is a form of prejudice (meaning "prejudgment") and discrimination. When people prejudge others, they hold certain attitudes, opinions, and beliefs about others without adequate knowledge. When these attitudes, opinions, and beliefs become actualized into behavior, the result is discrimination.

During the past few years, we have witnessed significant discrimination result from homophobia. Specifically, as gay/lesbian/bisexual persons have become more visible, state and local bodies, such as school boards, increasingly have promulgated antigay legislation and policies.

> [A] new legislative trend seems to have grown in the 1990s: affirmatively antigay legislation. . . . [I]n 1984 only five antigay measures were introduced in state legislatures. By comparison, in 1994 there were twenty-four antigay bills pending in state bodies. In the early months of 1995, eleven antigay bills had been introduced. . . . The fact is that an ever-more-specific and sophisticated legislative backlash to gay rights is under way at the state and local level.[7]

For example, in my state of New Hampshire a 1986 law makes it illegal for anyone with a gay or lesbian household member to become an adoptive or foster parent. Similarly, in September 1995, a New Hampshire high school teacher was fired for attempting to use in her classes two highly respected books that contained gay or lesbian characters. Thus, attitudes (prejudices) have become law (discrimination).

Such laws, policies, and legal actions are the products of unfounded fears about gay and lesbian people (for example, that being around us or reading about us is somehow harmful to children). There are no facts, statistics, or scientific evidence to support the views that gay/lesbian/bisexual people are any better or worse parents than heterosexual ones; that being around gay/lesbian/bisexual people causes homosexuality, any more than being around straight people causes heterosexuality; or that reading about gay and lesbian characters affects sexual orientation. In fact, there is compelling research to show that heterosexual men molest children of both genders more often than gay/lesbian/bisexual persons do.[8] Nonetheless, the law in New Hampshire regarding adoptive and foster parents remains on the books. Sadly, the result is that many children who need homes are denied access to loving people who want to adopt or serve as foster parents.

Despite research, education, and work toward justice, this and other forms of prejudice and discrimination continue to exist. Often even the best educational efforts do not abate prejudice. According to Warren Blumenfeld and Diane Raymond, this has to do with the origins of prejudice:

> Prejudice and discrimination can be tools used by the dominant group to maintain its control or power. Unless and until a minority group challenges this, this treatment may be viewed as being part of the natural order of things. The origins of prejudice are many and are extremely complex and include both the psychological makeup of the individual and the structural organization of the society.[9]

Although this book cannot treat all the numerous sources of prejudice and discrimination against lesbian/gay/bisexual persons in our society, two stand out and require more discussion.

First, discrimination against gay/lesbian/bisexual persons may be the result of what Sigmund Freud termed a "reaction formation"—the mechanism one uses to defend against an impulse in oneself by taking a firm stand against its expression in others. Specifically, people are frightened by their own non-heterosexual impulses and, therefore, seek to prevent them from being expressed or acknowledged by others.

Second, discrimination against gay/lesbian/bisexual persons serves a function similar to all prejudice and discrimination: It serves to maintain the economic control and power of the dominant group. Discrimination against gay/lesbian/bisexual persons reinforces the assumption that the traditional family unit, headed by the husband/father/breadwinner is the only acceptable unit or economic structure.[10]

In order to understand the experience and effects of prejudice and discrimination, one must understand that all forms of oppression and manifestations of discrimination share common elements and a common origin—economic and political power and control. In *Homophobia: A Weapon of Sexism*,[11] Suzanne Pharr asserts that there are many such common elements.

The first is the establishment of a defined norm or standard of rightness by which others are judged. Pharr asserts that the established norm does not necessarily represent a majority in numbers. Rather, it represents those who have the ability to exert power and control over others, institutionally as well as individually. Maintaining this control to establish norms requires the use of violence and the threat of violence.

Second, Pharr states that those who fall outside the norm of rightness are defined as "the other." This otherness is maintained through the combination of invisibility, the distortion of events, and stereotyping. Stereotyping and distortion lead to another common element of oppression, the tendency to blame victims for their own oppression. The goal of this element is to lead the victims toward an attitude of complicity with their oppression, thus believing it is deserved and should not be resisted.

The blaming of victims creates another common element for the oppressed—internalized oppression, a natural effect of taking in so many negative messages. Internalized oppression takes many forms, including self-hatred, depression, and self-abuse. Sometimes this internalization of oppression is acted out in forms of horizontal hostility; that is, expressing hostility toward another oppressed group rather than toward the oppressor. This all-too-disempowering phenomenon occurs regularly within the gay/lesbian/bisexual community as well as in other oppressed minorities. For example, gay men may express disdain toward transgendered persons, or Latinos and African Americans may vent anger at one another rather than at the sources of white heterosexist power.

Another major component of oppression is isolation, which occurs both in individuals and in groups. Related to isolation are the experiences of assimilation and tokenism, which are often manifest in the pressures to conform in culture and minimize distinctions in order to "fit" within a dominant group's experience and expectations. The final element, as described by Pharr, has to do with the oppressed group's needs, processing, and organizing for justice often being replaced by an emphasis on individual solutions. These components of oppression are examples of what Irvashi Vaid calls "mainstreaming rather than liberation."

> The limits of mainstreaming are equally evident today. The liberty we have won is incomplete, conditional, and ultimately revocable. All gay and lesbian people remain stigmatized and subject to violence; certain gay and lesbian people are freer than others. . . . A mainstream civil rights strategy cannot deliver genuine freedom of full equality for one fundamental reason: the goal of winning mainstream tolerance . . . differs from the goal of winning liberation or changing social institutions in a lasting, long-term way.[12]

I believe that it is critical for anyone seeking to understand the experience of lesbian/gay/bisexual persons to understand these common elements of oppression. In my experience as a pastor working in an emerging congregation that names itself as "a gay/straight justice-seeking community," I have witnessed these elements at play over and over again in the lives of many who begin to reach out to others. I have received phone calls from those who are too afraid to come to a worship service if it is publicly known that a gay/lesbian/bisexual group is meeting there. One woman spoke of her fear that the police would be sitting outside in their cars and would somehow harass the worshipers. One man told me that he feels so laden with emotional and spiritual guilt for his sexual orientation that he refuses to come to worship, even though he served as a deacon in a mainline congregation before "coming out" and would still like to be part of a worshipping congregation. At the same time, I have witnessed others who began to name their own internalized oppression and work through it within the context of community. They are now active leaders in the political and cultural movement for nondiscrimination in New Hampshire. We must acknowledge and address these elements of oppression if we are ever to be able to heal as a church or as a society.

The term *homophobia* was coined by psychotherapist Dr. George Weinberg in 1972. Weinberg begins *Society and the Healthy Homosexual* by stating that he "would never consider a patient healthy unless he [or she] had overcome . . . prejudice against homosexuality."[13] Weinberg expands this statement by describing the cost of this phobia to both heterosexual and homosexual persons. He cites the example of a father who upon hearing his son declare that he is gay, immediately pronounces the son sick, punches him, and forbids him ever to return to the house again. If we understand homosexuality as a illness, Weinberg says, then the father's distress looks reasonable, but his assault does not. People do not hit people because they are ill; people assault others because they are afraid. Hence the "phobia" as regards negative attitudes toward homosexuality.

Weinberg defines *homophobia* as "the dread of being in close quarters with homosexuals—and in the case of homosexuals themselves, self-loathing." He goes on to say that much has been written about homosexuality because it has been considered a problem. However, very little has been written about homophobia because "our unwarranted distress over homosexuality is not classified as a problem because it is still a majority point of view. Homophobia is still part of the conventional American attitude."[14]

The purposes that homophobia serves, or the reasons that it develops, have to do with the elements of oppression previously cited. However, there are more reasons and ways that this particular prejudice has developed over time. Dr. George Weinberg contends that there are five primary motives to homophobia: (1) the religious motive, (2) the secret fear of being homosexual, (3) repressed envy, (4) the threat to values, and (5) existence without vicarious immortality.[15]

1. *The religious motive:* The religious motive refers to the traditional Jewish and Christian laws, including biblical admonitions against spilling the seed, as well as a strict sexual code. Weinberg claims that the oppression of homosexuals became most atrocious when ecclesiastical powers gave their support to it. If one is to understand the early Jewish and Christian historical communities as religious systems within a society filled with competing religious systems, the purpose of these admonitions makes some sense. Specifically, the prohibition against spilling the seed reflected a concern for physical survival and procreation. At a time when survival was much more difficult, population growth was a key factor in maintaining the security, power, and place of any religion. In addition, this admonition against homosexual acts (since homosexuality as a part of the personality was not understood at that time) may have been a way to set boundaries to differentiate the Israelites clearly from surrounding pagan and nomadic cultures. Obviously, the religious, technological, and social circumstances are different today, obviating the need for this law. (I wonder what the law would have stated had the biblical writers lived in a time of overpopulation and dwindling resources.)

2. *The secret fear of being homosexual:* This fear has to do with the previously mentioned reaction formation, as defined by Freud, and the act of projecting one's fear onto the other. In systems thinking, one could interpret this as the system having become stuck in rigid patterns of interactions and identity. Essentially, this means that members of the system project cer-

tain ideas, feelings, and images onto other members, who in turn behave in ways concordant with the projections. As Salvador Minuchin, a family systems therapist, would say, the system is stuck in rigid stereotyped responses. This is a social or systemic version of projective identification and internalization of oppressive attitudes. For example, if gay/lesbian/bisexual persons within the church have been forced into the position of scapegoat for uncontained sexuality (projection), then they carry a significant amount of shame and guilt for the whole system (internalization). Through both positive (meaning active) and negative (meaning passive or absent) feedback, this position is confirmed and endures as patterns are reinforced and handed down from generation to generation. One grows up and is socialized within the church system knowing that gay/lesbian/bisexual persons are "not okay and are not us." Therefore, the roles continue, deeply imbedded in our social and individual psyches, enabling the projection of fear.

3. *Repressed envy:* In discussing this motive, Weinberg points to the threat that homosexuality places on sexist assumptions—especially in regard to male/female relationships. Again, the perspective of systems thinking is helpful to understand the power of roles, relationships, and pattered interactions. The system of mutual interaction between men and women is so ingrained in church and society that boundaries between them have become extremely rigid. Therefore, the envy that one member of the system may feel toward another who plays a different role is inexpressible and must go underground.

It is important to note here that these boundaries are held rigidly in place partly by patriarchal thinking and unequal positions of power within the institution. Although Weinberg limits his interpretation of this motive to envy of the other, I assert that the context of this envy has to do with the fear of loss of power and of men's domination over women in a sexist church and society. Structural family systems theory, as defined by Minuchin, states that roles are complementary. However, from a feminist perspective, this concept of complementarity does not necessarily mean equality; it only means that there are enduring patterns of position and interaction. These patterns and the power differential within them are connected to the repression and internalization of envy.

4. The threat to values: In naming the threat to values as a motive to homophobia, Weinberg claims that anyone who does not operate within the usual values system of a society is viewed as dangerous. Values serve to uphold the power dynamics, control, roles, structures, and boundaries of a system. Therefore, to threaten or even to vary from the normative values is seen as an act that could lead to the destruction of the system. In this light, *family values* is a code phrase for traditional systemic power, roles, and structures which continue to place gay/lesbian/bisexual persons in an oppressed position. Again, the connection between homophobia and sexism becomes clear in this area.

5. Existence without vicarious immortality. In discussing this motive, Weinberg asserts that people's negative reaction to gay and lesbian people without children often is motivated by their fear of death. This sounds like a modern-day correlation to the religious admonition against spilling the seed,[16] in its assumption that gay and lesbian sexual expression will somehow prevent procreation. In both cases, persons fear the dying out of culture and race.

This fear, however, is totally irrational in view of the technological and cultural realities of today's world. First, it assumes that lesbian and gay people cannot have children. Recently, I attend a shower for a lesbian who had adopted a baby. The living room was filled with newborns and latency-age children and their parents. The only adults in the room were lesbians. One need only attend a local pride march to see the importance of creating family, with and without children, in the lesbian/gay/bisexual community. Second, this fear assumes that giving birth and raising children are the only ways to assure the continuance of race and culture. Obviously, this assumption overlooks the generative qualities of art, music, literature, working for a more just and safe world, and the numerous other ways in which gay/lesbian/bisexual persons contribute to the longevity of life and culture.

In spite of these realities, this fear exists. The work of Murray Bowen in intergenerational family therapy helps to explain its power transference from one generation to the next. Within Bowen's framework, the importance of patterns, values, and belief systems, and their transference and endurance from one generation to the next is central. In addition, Bowen asserts that death and the family reaction to it are significant indicators of emotional health and well-being within any family system.

> Chief among all taboo subjects is death. A high percentage of people die alone, locked into their own thoughts which they cannot communicate to others. There are at least two processes in operation. One is the intrapsychic process in self which always involves some denial of death. The other is the closed relationship system. People cannot communicate the thoughts they do have, lest they upset the family or others.[17]

In the arena of homophobia, this interpsychic and systemic fear of death is played out through enduring sexist and heterosexist patterns. Neither the church nor society functions as an open system in regard to this issue. That is, persons do not readily give and receive feedback about these deep-seated concerns and fears; in other words, people just don't talk to each other about the scary stuff! Therefore, fears are often acted out in underground and unconscious manners. Thus, people do become limited in vision and stuck in traditional intergenerational patterns and assumptions. Essentially, this fear of death becomes a fear of the lack of generativity, assuming that birthing and raising children are the only ways to contribute to the future and assure the continuance of the system.

Understanding Weinberg's five primary motivations of homophobia may enable individuals to examine the purposes that homophobic attitudes are serving in their lives, and thereby empower them to work through these attitudes appropriately. These are also important systemic motivations, which provide a perspective on the role of homophobia within the church. Perhaps congregations, associations, conferences, and the national structure of the denomination can better understand homophobia in the church by looking at these potential functions of homophobia and how they are played out on many levels of the denomination.

Heterosexism

Closely associated with homophobia is heterosexism, which can be defined as

> the system by which heterosexuality is assumed to be the only acceptable and viable life option. . . . Because this norm is so pervasive, heterosexism is difficult to detect. . . . Heterosexism forces lesbians, gays, and bisexuals to struggle constantly against their own invisibility. . . . Heterosexism is discrimination by neglect, omission, and/or distortion, whereas often its more active partner—homophobia—is discrimination by intent and design.[18]

In "Coming Out and Relational Empowerment: A Lesbian Feminist Theological Perspective," Carter Heyward writes, "The dynamics of alienated power shape our eroticism as surely as they do the Pentagon budget." Heyward defines power as "the ability to move, effect, make a difference; the energy to create or destroy." In this definition, power is neither good nor bad; rather the purpose that it serves defines its goodness or badness. "Alienated power" is power that is "power-over (and) serves to further empower a few and disempower others."[19] It is the opposite of relational power. Heyward connects this alienated power with sexism and heterosexism in that its purpose is for a few to control others. She goes on to point out that heterosexism is the logical extension of sexism and serves the same purpose of controlling women's bodies and lives through this structuring of alienated power.

One can find numerous examples of heterosexism throughout our society. Perhaps the one that most painfully reminds me of the power of this system comes from a conversation that occurred around my own dinner table. At the time, I had been living with my partner and her children for two years and had been involved in a day-to-day relationship as a stepmother with the youngest child since she was two. Before buying a house and moving in together, we held two rituals—a marriage covenant between my partner and me, and a home and family blessing that included the children. We had many conversations with the children about our family and our "marriage." They had seemed to understand and be happy and well adjusted. One night at the dinner table, someone mentioned marriage, which prompted the youngest child to ask if her biological mother were getting married. My partner explained that she and I were already married. The child laughed and said, "Girls can only marry boys."

The way I understand this interaction is that despite the influence of her home life and her positive experience of living in a noncloseted lesbian family system, the heterosexist influences in our society were strong enough to permeate the boundaries of our home and negate this child's own life experience. The movies she watches, the stories she reads, the words and images of family at school, church, and in society are of heterosexual family units. Therefore, her own reality is denied and confused. Such is the power of heterosexism.

Manifestations of homophobia and heterosexism can be found socially, theologically, interpersonally, internally, or intra-psychically. Societal homophobia is becoming increasingly evident as groups organize across the country to deny even the possibility of basic civil and human rights to gay/lesbian/bisexual persons. However, even without this legalized discrimination, one does not have to look far to find evidence of social homophobia. Blumenfeld and Raymond cite eight manifestations of collective homophobia, or what they call "social codes of behavior." These are the denial of culture, the denial of popular strength, the fear of overvisibility, the conspiracy to silence, the creation of defined public spaces, the denial of self-labeling, negative symbolism, and limited social tolerance.[20]

Each of these "social codes of behavior" is reinforced through the power of the heterosexist system in society and church. First, the denial of culture is perhaps the most powerful negative feedback to gay/lesbian/bisexual persons about our place in the system. By and large, gay/lesbian/bisexual culture continues to be underground, except in some urban centers. History, art, and politics have been virtually silent about the contributions of gay/lesbian/bisexual people. Sadly, the AIDS epidemic brought to the public consciousness some of the contributions of gay artists in recent culture.

From a more social and contemporary perspective, access to gay/lesbian/bisexual culture is very limited. Many people in our society would suggest that it does not even exist—especially in their own home towns. They are wrong. Even in a conservative, rural state like New Hampshire, where an office of the Christian Coalition stands on Main Street near the capitol, there are gay and lesbian social, support, political, and religious groups. There are networks of gay and lesbian or gay/lesbian "friendly" professional and service providers. I am sure that most of my own neighbors would be truly surprised to know how many of us are here, and that we have a life and a community.

Throughout much of its history, the church has continued to support this denial of culture through the same silence about history, art, politics, and spirituality. Perhaps this is one of the reasons that the Open and Affirming (ONA) movement is so critical. Through it, heterosexual as well as gay/lesbian/bisexual persons are learning about gay culture and are beginning to accommodate it within the system. Only time will tell whether this will be simply another avenue of mainstreaming and supporting the status quo or a step toward true and long-lasting liberation.

The denial of popular strength/support is closely related to and dependent on the visibility of gay/lesbian/bisexual culture. Popular strength has begun to emerge in such events as gay/lesbian/bisexual pride days and the marches on Washington. The significance of this, from a psychological perspective, is that this emergence of strength has resulted from gay/lesbian/bisexual persons naming and externalizing oppressive internalizations about themselves, stepping out of predescribed roles and boundaries, and forming new power alignments and patterns of interactions.

In the church, such popular strength may have to come from a realignment of relationships such as occurs when persons refuse to be silent and complicit in their oppression. This happens in the forming of new church starts, coalitions, and support groups. Certainly, realigning oneself places one outside the traditional structures of power, but it also creates the opportunity for new feedback, permeable boundaries, and creative structures and opportunities for ministry.

The fear of overvisibility, the conspiracy to silence, and the creation of defined public spaces are all closely intertwined both in church and society. Each of these serves to reinforce the role of perceived powerlessness of lesbian/gay/bisexual persons within the system, as well as to emphasize the void of negative feedback. How many times have we heard "Whatever gay/lesbian/bisexual persons do in their own bedrooms is their business, as long as they don't flaunt it"? Whenever I have asked someone what they mean by "flaunting," they describe behaviors commonly associated with the norms of heterosexuality (i.e., wearing wedding rings, holding hands, talking about one's spouse, etc.). When I came out while pastoring a church, several members came to me and said something like, "We knew that you were a lesbian, but why did you have to go and talk about it?"

The denial of self-labeling, negative symbolism, and limited social tolerance also serve to maintain the role and position of invisibility and powerlessness of lesbian/gay/bisexual persons. Terms such as *dyke* and *faggot* are obviously used as put-downs, objectifications, threats, and sometimes as preludes to physical violence in our society. I remember a conversation with a parishioner a few years ago in which she expressed her distress that her five-year-old son had come home from kindergarten playing "smear the queer." Hatred is programmed early in our society. Even as a very "out" lesbian, I remain keenly aware of the limits of tolerance (as compared to liberation) and how far one can push these limits without risking violence and the threat of violence, even in the church. It is also important to note that because we live in a heterosexist and violent society, there are no precautions we can take to ensure our safety. We are all at risk.

I believe that these manifestations of homophobia are important to an understanding of the experience of lesbian/gay/bisexual persons in our society and in the church. If the church is seen as a subsystem within the larger society or suprasystem, these issues become imperative, because they are as evident in the society as they are throughout the institution of the church. Again, I would encourage church members to address these issues at all levels, asking how the church is complicit in homophobic and heterosexist patterns and structures.

Specifically, the culture and strength of lesbian/gay/bisexual persons within the church had been virtually invisible except on a national level before the Open and Affirming (ONA) movement in the United Church of Christ and related movements in other denominations. The very presence of nonheterosexuals within the institution, let alone in roles of leadership, has been denied for generations.

In addition, it has been my experience that the ONA movement does raise peoples' fears and biases in regard to the fear of overvisibility, a conspiracy of silence, and negative symbolism. For example, after I came out publicly and was serving as pastor of a local church, I heard some parishioners voice their concern that if they declared themselves "Open and Affirming, all kinds of homosexuals would be showing up." I remember one man saying "We'll take a few, you know, our share, but no more." At this same time, several deacons confirmed that we were becoming known as "the queer church" because we had an openly lesbian pastor and a few lesbian members. (I wondered why we were not known as "the left-handed church" since the pastor was also overtly left-handed as were a minority of church members.)

In "The Respectable Gay Men and Lesbians: A Negotiated-order Approach to the Inclusion of Gay Men and Lesbians in the Congregational Life of Liberal Protestantism," Christopher Carrington confirms the power of these social codes. Carrington studies the Open and Affirming study process in a liberal, highly educated, wealthy, urban congregation. One of Carrington's conclusions is that the congregants' vote to declare themselves Open and Affirming was easier because the lesbians and gay men among them fit in with the predominant lifestyle and expectations of the congregation.

> Successful integration into the congregation practically required a higher education. Gay people did not object to this, in fact, they embodied it. . . . Members of First Church, like many in American Society, were uncomfortable with ambiguous expressions of gender identity. . . . [G]ay people not only accepted these expectations, they emphatically embraced them and were clear to draw a distinction between themselves and "those" gays out in the world who engaged in gender-bending or drag.[21]

As Blumenfeld and Raymond suggest, intellectual tolerance does not equate with liberation.

Internalized Homophobia

Related to the social manifestations of homophobia are the manifestations of internalized homophobia. In "Internalized Homophobia: Identifying and Treating the Oppressor Within," authors Margolies, Becker, and Jackson-Brewer state that "The oppressive and prejudiced environment takes root, feeding on histories, issues, and the unique social conditions of each individual. This internal oppressor cannot be identified, re-evaluated, and worked through without first clearly understanding the role of social deviance and the reality of its danger to the individual."[22] In other words, being different and being "out" are scary, exhausting, and risky at best. Therefore, since lesbian/gay/bisexual persons have the options to be "in" by passing as straight and not risking public identification as "deviant," many choose to remain closeted.

Through my pastoral work, I have come to agree with these authors that it is very difficult—if not impossible—for lesbian/gay/bisexual persons to understand fully our own negative attitudes, frustrations, and fears without first understanding what society has done to us. This is not meant for the sake of blaming or venting, but as the only way of understanding the true roots of our distress and the way to a healthy self. One must understand the social roots of oppression and the ways in which one can still assume responsibility in order not to be victimized by the internalized oppression.

Many lesbian couples have come to me for counseling when their relationships were in trouble. I have found repeatedly that these couples lack the supportive social structures that help to stabilize any family unit. Lesbian and gay couples, much more than heterosexual couples, are often so isolated as couples that trying to stay together through difficulties can seem overwhelming. After all, where does support for same-sex couples really come from? It certainly is not present in the legal, financial, employment, social, or religious structures of society. It rarely comes from families of origin (who are often relieved to have their prejudices "confirmed" in the troubles of their gay/lesbian/bisexual relatives). Gay and lesbian couples must create our own support systems and structures out of our own community and life resources.

One of the manifestations of internalized homophobia is the seeming lack of respect we have, as a community, for our own intimate relationships. Although gay and lesbian weddings, covenant ceremonies, and union services (there is no unified name or understanding of this ritual) once were rare, they currently are becoming more common. This, in itself, is a clear sign that we are honoring our needs for ritual and relationships more highly.

Every time I work with a couple in preparing for some type of covenanting ceremony, we discuss the symbolic and practical significance of legalizing the relationship through legal partnerships, powers of attorney, etc. I give them examples of necessary documents along with the names of lawyers to help them with the process. Although marriage automatically confers legal benefits on heterosexual couples, lesbian and gay couples have to initiate discussion of such issues. So far, every couple with whom I have worked has agreed that this is important. Nonetheless, at this point, I am aware of only one couple that has actually followed through with anything more than the power of attorney at this time of passage. After being together for some time, many gay and lesbian couples will buy property and/or create some type of legalized agreement. However, it is as if the internalized message devaluing the validity and longevity of gay and lesbian relationships is so powerful that we ourselves need to pass the test of time before we take ourselves seriously.

This lack of initial follow-through does not, I believe, stem from a political commitment not to get "trapped" in the legalities of the patriarchal culture that surrounds us. Instead, I believe it arises from a lack of self-esteem, internalized feelings of guilt and shame, an unspoken belief that "we probably won't make it anyway," a fear of being legally "outed," and a shortage of economic resources (even feminist lawyers cost a lot of money).

Margolies, Becker, and Jackson-Brewer go on to list eight psychological manifestations of internalized homophobia in lesbians:

1. Fear of discovery.
2. Discomfort with obvious "fags" and "dykes."
3. Rejection/denigration of all heterosexuals.
4. Feeling superior to heterosexuals.
5. Belief that lesbians are not different from heterosexual women.
6. An uneasiness with the idea of children being raised in a lesbian home.
7. Restricting attractions to unavailable women, heterosexuals, and those already partnered.
8. Short-term relationships.[23]

I find this list to be very helpful in my pastoral counseling work with lesbian/gay/bisexual persons. If, through the power of homophobia, lesbian/gay/bisexual persons have internalized the image of themselves as the bad and projected the good onto heterosexual persons, then the guilt and shame inherent in their same-gender relationship can overpower their desire to honor the relational commitment they have made. Therefore, it follows that an important goal to work toward is that of empowering lesbian/gay/bisexual persons to name these manifestations of internalized homophobia and withdraw their internal and external projections, so that when a problem or crisis arises within a relationship, they may deal with the relational issues and not hide them within a fog of homophobia. In the same manner, individuals, couples, families, and communities are empowered when they can name the role of internalized homophobia in interpersonal, vocational, spiritual, and emotional struggles in order to facilitate healing and growth.

Another psychologically significant issue related to internalized homophobia concerns the many questions around "the closet": whether to stay in or come out. As one who was in for quite a while and has now been out for several years, I have come to know profoundly that the state of one's mental health (especially around issues of self-esteem, guilt and shame, and depression) depends on one's ability to claim who one is and to let go of the many added psychological defenses necessary to maintain life in the closet. However, psychological health cannot be addressed in a vacuum apart from sociological realities (i.e., the system within which we all live). Therefore, one must weigh the cost and face the realities of the threats of job loss, violence, harassment, and loss of children and family.

In the Stone Center paper "Issues in Psychotherapy with Lesbian Women," Dr. Nanette Gartrell states the importance of "coming out" for lesbians, both as therapists and clients: "Maintaining secrecy about one's lesbianism demands psychic energy, and it is injurious to self-esteem. . . . [G]enerally a lesbian experiences marked improvement in psychological well-being as she sheds the burden of secrecy."[24]

In addition to affirming the importance of coming out, Gartrell also affirms that coming out is a process and way of being that is a choice for every day.

> Although it is often tempting to avoid disclosing one's lesbianism to people whom one does not know well, I remind clients that they are likely to come away from every situation in which they have deferred to heterosexist assumptions feeling bad. Generally, the decision to conceal one's lesbianism . . . is accompanied by an internalization of the negative attitudes which one assumes other people would express if one's lesbianism were acknowledged. . . . [B]eing out allows one to externalize rather than internalize the anger one feels in response to homophobia.[25]

Carter Heyward confirms the significance in the act of coming out by describing it in her writing not only as a step toward "personal authenticity" but also as a "step into a posture of social and political deviance and resistance . . . a remarkable process of relational empowerment."[26]

Given the effects of the internalization of homophobia, it becomes clear that being out enhances psychological well-being. When one is out, the added layers of defense mechanisms may be let go, allowing more appropriate individuation, acceptance, understanding, and creation of the solid self, as well as celebration of oneself as a beloved child of God. The difficulty in this process is the social cost of coming out, which may include loss of job, loss of family (including children), and even loss of physical safety.

During the past four years of pastoring a small, rural, and primarily gay/lesbian/bisexual congregation, I have worked with four women who have lost or potentially may lose custody and/or visitation with their children upon their coming out. I have worked with two gay men who were physically beaten by straight men in separate incidents, one youth who attempted suicide after coming out to his family, and more than a few lesbians and gay men who felt their jobs were threatened because their employer might have discovered their sexual orientation. Thus gay/lesbian/bisexual people are always in a double-bind. We need to be out in order to gain the greatest psychological and spiritual health and well-being. However, this very act places us at risk socially, economically, and physically.

One source of confusion for lesbian/gay/bisexual Christians is the apparent contradiction between the church's words about healing and wholeness for God's children and its collusion in the spiritual and psychological oppression of lesbian/gay/bisexual persons. Specifically, to come out in the church is to risk exile from the body of Christ. "Out" persons, especially pastors, almost inevitably lose some position of power that they had attained when closeted. Depending on the congregation and denomination, this may range from a particular parish position to ordination itself. I have recently had conversations with two very talented gay pastors, both of whom highly affirmed by their congregations. By all outward signs they are successful. Nonetheless, they described to me their gut-wrenching pain, their lack of self esteem, their feelings of guilt, shame, and fear. They described their fantasies of coming out and their fear that if they do so they will be forced to resign, facing unemployment and the vocational crisis of being expelled from their call. They feel that they must choose between themselves and their vocation, which is profoundly accurate in psychological and spiritual terms. To be human is to seek relationship. Yet, if we bring our full selves to others, we risk losing the very relationships that help us to be human in the first place.

This crisis occurs within the very church that preaches "release to the captives" and the love of God's children who are all made in God's image. That this contradiction persists despite the ONA/Welcoming Congregations movement points to just how antithetical the church really is to spiritual and psychological liberation.

Everything that has been stated so far about the role and effects of homophobia and heterosexism in society can also be said of the church. Homophobia and heterosexism come from similar origins, function in similar roles, and serve similar purposes whether one is talking about the structure of power in society or in the church. In the words of Warren Blumenfeld and Diane Raymond, "History has shown that there exists a symbiotic relationship between religious and secular teachings on the issue of homosexuality, with one both influencing and used to justify the other."[27]

This relationship between social and religious views on homosexuality is described in detail in the work of John Boswell, who states that where society has been tolerant of lesbian/gay/bisexual persons, so has the predominant religion, and vice versa. For example, he asserts that in ancient cities gay people enjoyed significant toleration before even religious nonconformists. However, in the modern Western world, attention to issues of intolerance of sexual orientation comes long after issues of race or religion have been raised. Boswell states that this is related to the society's social structure, which is often closely connected to the structure of religion.[28]

In addition, Boswell points out the connection between religious intolerance and sexual intolerance:

> Most societies, for instance, which freely tolerate religious diversity also accept sexual variation, and the fate of Jews and gay people has almost been identical throughout European history. . . . The same laws which oppressed Jews oppressed gay people; the same groups bent on eliminating Jews tried to wipe out homosexuality, . . . and even the same methods of propaganda were used.[29]

This connection between religious intolerance and sexual intolerance is also described in the recent book *Stranger at the Gate*, by Mel White. Reverend White spent most of his youth and adult years in conservative, evangelical Christian circles. He quickly rose to the top, and became a ghost writer for Jerry Falwell, Oliver North, Pat Robertson, and others. In *Stranger at the Gate*, White vividly tells of his own painful struggle to live as a heterosexual. He writes from his perspective as a previous "insider" of the conservative religious and political movement and makes some important connections.

> During the 1990's, when the religious right shifted the focus of their fund-raising appeals from the "evil communist empire" to "the homosexual agenda for the destruction of America," I began collecting samples of their terrible lies against us. One . . . stated simply: "Declaration of War . . . Official Notice." Jerry Falwell was officially declaring war against gay and lesbian people. Why? Because, according to Jerry, homosexuals "have a godless, humanistic scheme for our nation—a plan which will destroy America's traditional moral values. He went on to claim that our "goal" as gays and lesbians was the "complete elimination of God and Christianity for American society."
>
> It was the same tired, old lie that Adolf Hitler and Heinrich Himmler had used in 1936 when they created a Reich Central Office for the Combating of Homosexuality and Abortion. . . . In a February 18, 1937, speech to the office corps of Hitler's storm troopers, Himmler warned "that if we continue to have this bur-

den (of homosexuality) on Germany, without being able to fight it, then that is the end of Germany, and the end of the Germanic world."[30]

History teaches us that intolerance of any kind is one of the most dangerous threats to humanity.

It is hoped that through the material in this chapter, the reader gained has a clear awareness of sexual orientation and the power of homophobia and heterosexism in the church and society. To summarize, homophobia and heterosexism are powerful forces in both church and society. Systemically, the interrelationship of church and society continues to promote homophobia within each. In addition, the intergenerational transmittal of values, patterns, and roles has included, for generations, handing down homophobia and heterosexism. Therefore, we are dealing with issues that are intrapsychically, interpsychically, and systemically very deep. Homophobia and heterosexism are manifested spiritually and theologically when the church proclaims a mixed message: calling the faithful to celebrate our creation as God's children, made in God's image, seeking the liberation of all people, while condemning lesbian/gay/bisexual persons to silence about who we really are and threatening us with exile from the loving community if we speak the truth of our creation. Homophobia is manifested psychologically when lesbian/gay/bisexual persons internalize the shame and guilt projected onto us by heterosexist attack on our self-esteem, forcing us to feel as though we must split our public selves from our private selves in order to survive. Psychological homophobia also takes a toll on heterosexual persons through the repression and projection of same-gender sexual impulses, which inhibits the development of a fully integrated sexual self.

Homophobia and heterosexism are manifested ethically when lesbian/gay/bisexual persons and relationships are presumed to be sick, bad, evil, sinful, or lesser than heterosexual ones. This prevents the making of covenantal relationships or the living of lives based on an ethic of love and justice.

Understanding and addressing homophobia in the church and society are sacred and significant undertakings. To confront homophobia is to confront the power structures that keep us alienated from one another—whether we are lesbian, gay, bisexual, or heterosexual—and to move us away from postures of alienation and disconnection to postures of empowerment and mutual relation. To confront homophobia is to take on and challenge the internal voices that tell us there are certain rules and roles for gender-appropriate behavior, and that to break these rules invites societal shame and the possibility of violent retaliation.

To confront homophobia and heterosexism is to join with the lives of others oppressed by the patriarchal system of power and control and to confirm that, indeed, "no one is free while others are oppressed." To confront homophobia in the church is to begin to join with others as we affirm the depth and breadth of God's creative power, for only in our diversity do we see the fullness of God's image.

While serving as pastor of Spirit of the Mountains during the past four years, I have heard the stories of lesbian mothers losing custody, of a gay man being beaten by a police officer, of a teenage boy being expelled from his home when he came out to his parents, of four gay and lesbian persons losing their jobs because of their sexual orientation, of friends continuing to grieve the death of two lesbians murdered in a violent hate crime, and of a gay youth-outreach worker's ongoing pain over the suicides of so many gay/lesbian/bisexual young people. These are only some of the stories related by some of the people connected with a small community in New England. To see this happening throughout our nation and world is to see the evil that comes from homophobia and heterosexism. Yet see it and face it we must. To confront homophobia is to save lives and resist evil.

Questions for Discussion

1. How could you, as an individual, clarify your own use of terms and definitions regarding sexual orientation? How can

your church be certain you share similar language understandings so that you are not misunderstood when discussing your own beliefs and/or experiences?

2. How would you describe homophobia and heterosexism?
How do you witness and experience them today in church
and society?

3. How do you see the motivations of homophobia as set forth
by George Weinberg functioning in yourself, your congregation, your denomination, your society?

4. What new understandings do you have of your own internalized homophobia? Can you give examples of ways that it
is manifest and operates within your self-identity, your relationships with others, your social/political worldviews? What
early memories do you have that might explain the origin of
this homophobia?

5. How can you begin to work through your own internalized
homophobia? What can your local church do?

2···

Where We Are, Where We Have Been, and Where We Are Going: A Brief Overview of the Gay/Lesbian/Bisexual Movement in Mainline Churches

On October 14, 1979, I had an experience that changed my life forever. At the age of twenty-one, I attended the first National March on Washington for Lesbian and Gay Rights. Were there one hundred thousand, two hundred thousand, or five hundred thousand people there? No one seems to know for sure. For me, a whole new world was there—a world I had never known about or even dreamed existed. I remember traveling from my home in Nashville, Tennessee, to Washington, D.C., in a very small Toyota with two wonderful gay men (two of my first gay friends, both of whom have since died from complications due to AIDS). As we drove through the night, I remember wondering what lay before me and what my parents would think if they knew where I was going! We arrived on the morning of the march and planned to leave that same evening to return home. At the time, I knew no one else there; however since then, I have discovered that some of my good friends were also there that day. As we parked and walked toward the gathering place, I remember being joyfully shocked and overwhelmed by the many gay and lesbian people I saw on the streets. As we walked onto the mall, where individuals and groups were gathering, I stood still in amazement and just took it all in. There were gay and lesbian groups from every imaginable location and walk of life. Today, when I am surprised by the intensity of someone's feeling when he or she begins to come out and connect with other gay/lesbian/bisexual persons, I am taken back to that day, some seventeen years ago, when my world changed forever.

A few weeks before the march, I had entered a master's program in social work at the University of Tennessee. For years I had planned on entering seminary, being ordained, and serving in parish ministry. However, when I came out to myself during my junior year of college, I needed to distance myself from the church. The next year, I decided to apply for social work school rather than theological school. I told my family and friends that I believed God was calling me to be in more direct contact with low-income and disenfranchised people than most parish ministry would allow. The real reason was that I felt unable to address the church's (any church's) homophobia on my own. I didn't know that there was help or support and that, in fact, I was not alone.

So here I was, the new social work student at her first march in Washington, D.C., and the first booth I saw (after watching the San Francisco Pride Marching Band in astonishment for a while) was a national organization for gay and lesbian social workers. I think I ran to that booth, picked up their literature, and spoke for a few minutes with a very nice man. From there, I wandered up and down the mall, seeing organizations from virtually every profession and trade. Each one caught my eye; however, I was truly amazed by the presence of religious groups and organizations. Now I cannot remember precisely which denominations were present, but in that moment I did realize the power of the slogan, "We Are Everywhere." In fact, gay, lesbian, bisexual, and transgendered people *are* everywhere—in every denomination and every parish. The church is also everywhere, sometimes working for justice and inclusivity and sometimes working against it.

Nearly fourteen years later, on April 23, 1993, I attended the third National March on Washington with a delegation from Spirit of the Mountains, the predominantly gay/lesbian/bisexual and affirming congregation that I pastor in Concord, New Hampshire. This time, Sunday morning began with a celebration of worship, filled to overflowing, at an Open and Affirming United Church of Christ congregation. The UCC delegation then marched together to join the estimated one million participants. One church member called it the "Stand on Washington," because it was so crowded that we did not move for several hours. During those hours, we stood with many other religious groups to take our place in line. There were organizations from the Disciples of Christ, the United Methodists, the Mennonites, the Quakers, the Unitarian Universalists, the American Baptists, the Southern Baptists, and others. I remember going from one group to another, greeting old and new friends, all gathered to march for liberation with the strength and source of our faith. I felt as though I had been invited to the community hour from heaven—a Sunday noon on the lawn in the warmth of beautiful sunshine, with God's finest angels and saints gathered together!

The gay/lesbian/bisexual movement for justice and liberation in the church had been very active and growing in vision, numbers, and strength in the interim between these two marches. Thus, in 1993, the religious presence was large, powerful, and celebrative. In addition, this movement had been both prophetic and supportive prior to the first march and continues to be so today.

Although in this chapter I can only provide a brief description of the lesbian/gay/bisexual Christian historical movement, some helpful resources are available for those who wish to make further inquiry. *Open Hands,* an ecumenical publication supported by the Welcoming Congregations movement (predominantly that of the United Methodist's Reconciling Congregation program) and by individual subscriptions, provides an invaluable resource for anyone wanting to become involved and/or know more about gay/lesbian/bisexual Christians. Two issues, in particular, provide a historical overview of the movement. "Growing in Faith: the Lesbian/Gay Christian Movement"[1] provides a time line and overview of the movement from 1964 to 1989. "Welcoming Churches: a Growing Ecumenical Movement"[2] looks at the movement by which churches and denominational bodies grow in ministry with gay/lesbian/bisexual persons through this particular program and process. An excellent resource paper by James D. Anderson of Rutgers University and Presbyterians for Lesbian and Gay Concerns, "The Lesbian and Gay Liberation Movement in the Churches of the United States, 1969–1993, with Special Reference to Presbyterians for Lesbian and Gay concerns, 1974–1993,"[3] describes the movement throughout several different denominations and nondenominational groups. These resources, along with personal interviews and materials from denominational organizations, have been the primary sources of information for this chapter.

Finally, if one is seeking information about early Christianity and homosexuality, the work of historian John Boswell is thorough and clear. His *Christianity, Social Tolerance, and Homosexuality; Gay People in Western Europe from the Beginning of the Christian Era to the Fourteenth Century*[4] and *Same-Sex Unions in Premodern Europe*[5] are both excellent resources.

In most Protestant denominations, the decade of the 1970s marked the coming together of the organized movement for advocacy and support. However, significant developments during the 1960s laid the groundwork for the organizing of the 1970s.

Often people trace the beginning of the movement to the Council of Religion and the Homosexual, which began in 1964. This ecumenical council was born out of a conference organized by the Reverend Ted McIlvenna in San Francisco. The purpose of this conference was to foster dialogue between the homophile organizations and the clergy from four different denominations (UMC, UCC, the Lutheran Church in America, and the Protestant Episcopal Church), as well as to educate church leaders about gay and lesbian concerns. The meeting began with these ministers immersing themselves in the gay community with weekend touring of gay bars and other community locales, followed by a three-day retreat. From this emerged the Council on Religion and the Homosexual (CRH), whose goals were orienting clergy to gay and lesbian life, encouraging congregations to listen to gay and lesbian people, coming to new understandings of religion and homosexuality, communicating accurate and objective information on homosexuality through the church press, training clergy to deal effectively as counselors in the area of sexuality, and speaking out on pertinent laws and policies.

In 1964, this council was the only place in which visible work was being done on homosexuality and religion. Through its forums, publications, and networks, gay and lesbian Christians began to come together ecumenically and within their own denominations. In 1975, when successful networking and organizing had begun to take place within denominations, the council—under the leadership of the Reverend Bill Johnson, a UCC minister—decided to disband.

Ever since the 1960s, gay/lesbian/bisexual persons have taken two primary directions in relation to the institutional church. One has been to remain within one's own denomination, working for justice through the development of advocacy and support groups. This is akin to the words a friend of mine once spoke: "I'm not leaving. They're gonna have to kick me out if they want to get rid of me!" The other direction has been to move outside of denominational structures to create churches and ministries aimed at the particular needs of lesbian/gay/bisexual persons. The best known of these is the Universal Fellowship of Metropolitan Community Churches. In 1968, the Reverend Troy Perry chose not to remain within the evangelical/pentecostal churches and instead founded the UFMCC in his living room. Since then it has grown immensely, with nearly three hundred congregations in over seventeen nations (and perhaps more by the time this is published). The UFMCC has sought membership in the National Council of Churches but, so far, has been denied. Today, some individuals and groups have combined these approaches by organizing congregations that focus on the gay/lesbian/bisexual community while remaining within denominational structures.

Beginning in 1970, gay and lesbian groups began to organize: advocating, networking, supporting individuals, providing educational material, and seeking just policy changes (and often trying to minimize damage). Three denominations in particular led the way in the early days of the gay and lesbian Christian movement and continue to do so today: the Unitarian-Universalist Association, the Friends (Quakers), and the United Church of Christ. On a denominational level, each of these communions has consistently offered clear public support of gay and lesbian persons in church and society. For example, in 1970, the Unitarian Universalist Association General Assembly adopted a resolution calling for an end to discrimination against gays and lesbians in law enforcement, civil services, and the military. By this time, the Friends had been dialoguing about homosexuality for several years. In 1963, the publication of the pamphlet "Toward a Quaker View of Sex" sparked significant discussion as a result of its candid and direct approach to sexuality and homosexuality. In 1972, Rev. Bill Johnson, the first openly gay man to be ordained by a mainline Protestant denomination, began his ministry in the United Church of Christ.

It is sad to note that even though these denominations have led the movement in many ways, homophobia is still a reality within each of them. Within the past week, I have heard of a lesbian minister in the UUA receiving threatening mail, a Friends congregation being called into question by the local association for performing the marriage of a lesbian couple (even though the first same-sex marriage took place in 1987 under the care of the Morningside Meeting in New York City). I have also recently spoken to an "out" lesbian UCC minister who has been searching more than two years for a congregation that will call her. The discrepancies between national policy and local practices are sometimes overwhelming. (These will be addressed in chapter 3).

Parallel to the steps taken by these three denominations, most other denominations began to sit precariously on a very narrow fence, a place they still occupy today. This fence seems to be placed somewhere between affirming gay and lesbian civil rights (or at least the right to be free from violence) and denying gay and lesbian persons full participation in the church. In these churches, openly gay or lesbian persons cannot be ordained and, in some cases, cannot serve as church officers or on church councils. Nonetheless, these prohibitions have not stopped gay/lesbian/bisexual persons and their supporters from organizing for support and advocacy.

In 1970, several steps were taken to support and advocate for gay and lesbian people across denominations. For example,

Dignity, an organization for gay/lesbian Catholics, was founded in San Francisco. Since that time, Dignity has grown tremendously, with chapters in most major cities and many small towns. The Unitarian-Universalist Association Gay Caucus was also created, and an ecumenical gay seminarians; group was founded at the Graduate Theological Union in the greater San Francisco area.

Soon after this, efforts began to deal with the concerns of gay and lesbian persons throughout several denominations. Some of this activity was supportive and prophetic about the place of lesbians and gay men in the church, while much of it was devastating. Specifically, the Lutheran Church in America declared homosexuality to be "a departure from the heterosexual nature of God's creation," and the United Methodist Church adopted its infamous line, "We do not condone the practice of homosexuality and consider this practice incompatible with Christian teaching."

At the same time, Rev. Bill Johnson was ordained as an openly gay clergyman and began the UCC Gay Caucus. Soon after this, the American Baptist Gay Caucus, the Presbyterian Gay Caucus, and Integrity (Episcopalians) were founded. In 1972 the Metropolitan Community Temple, the first lesbian/gay synagogue was opened in Los Angeles. Other steps were also being taken at that time which aided the progress of gay and lesbian concerns, including the publishing of gay/lesbian denominational newsletters, magazines, and books. Also caucuses such as Evangelicals Concerned and the lesbian/gay Seventh Day Adventists were being formed. Ellen Barrett, an "out" lesbian and copresident of Integrity was ordained into the Episcopal priesthood, and Malcolm Boyd, another Episcopal priest, came out in his book *Take Off the Masks*. Thus, by the end of the 1970s, denominations as diverse as the Seventh-Day Adventists and the United Methodists had gay and lesbian caucuses. There were a few (albeit very few) openly gay and lesbian clergypersons, and an increasing number of publications and books were being circulated by the movement.

At the same time, many denominations were creating and implementing task forces and study groups on the topic of homosexuality. However, the majority of these ended in heated debate with pronouncements attempting to "separate the sin from the sinner." In other words, most churches (excluding the few that were making positive changes) were trying to tell gay and lesbian people to come to church and give of ourselves to the church but to leave our sexuality on the doorstep outside. Sadly, this is what many gay, lesbian, and bisexual people have done and continue to do today. We bring our spirituality into the sanctuary on Sunday morning while our sexuality remains in the "secular" world, an unnatural and dangerous split.

This religious movement for support, justice, and advocacy in the 1970s interwove with the social and political steps being taken throughout society at the time. The "Stonewall generation" was also organizing support and social groups, participating in pride marches, seeking to remove the sodomy laws from some states, and working for visibility and antidiscrimination.

At the same time, major cultural and political backlashes began to occur, often fueled by religious fervor (as they are fueled today). Singer and product pitchwoman Anita Bryant led a much-publicized crusade against gay and lesbian people by seeking to repeal the antidiscrimination legislation in Dade County, Florida. I still remember reading about and seeing some of the violence that came out of that time—especially one bumper sticker that was supposed to be funny: "Kill a Queer for Christ." It was also during this time, on November 27, 1978, that Harvey Milk, the first openly gay member of the board of supervisors in San Francisco, was assassinated. When gay/lesbian/bisexual people began to be visible, the opposition became organized and ruthless (as is the case today), usually proclaiming religious rhetoric as their source of power and belief.

Throughout the decade of the 1980s, the gay and lesbian Christian movement continued to solidify, expand, network, and speak out for recognition and justice in church and society. New gay and lesbian groups were being formed in such denominations as the Christian Scientists and the Mennonites. Meanwhile, many existing groups were networking to build a cooperative movement, which continues today. Lesbian and gay seminarian conferences and other ecumenical groups came into being and still exist in one form or another.

Gay and lesbian clergy of many denominations came out in an effort to speak the truth of our lives and communicate to our brothers and sisters in the church that we are not strangers, but in fact, members and leaders of the body of Christ. Depending on the polity of one's particular denomination, to come out often meant being denied ordination, or loosing the ability to be reappointed for a position in ministry. For some, it meant losing the office of ordination or a job, while for others it meant enduring harassment or even losing membership in their church. Coming out in the church has been a significant step of recognition and liberation. However, many have paid a heavy price in doing so.

Another major focus of the 1980s was the beginning of the Welcoming Church movement. We will address this movement in greater detail later in this chapter, but it is important to note here that in the mid-1980s several denominational caucuses began their own Welcoming Church movement, often as a way for local churches to proclaim their faith in spite of their denomination's position.

One cannot reflect on the religious and/or secular gay and lesbian movement of the 1980s without acknowledging the profound losses and effects of the AIDS epidemic. Many important leaders in the church and society became infected and have since died. Denominational caucuses often have been overwhelmed with grief, and resources that once had been focused on justice and liberation were now being turned to address the harsh realities of AIDS and HIV. The emotional, spiritual, political, financial, and social effects of AIDS cannot be overstated. For more information about this, I suggest that you contact your denominational AIDS ministry.

Finally, during the first half of the 1990s, the work of creating justice for gay/lesbian/bisexual persons within the church has continued to grow and expand. The Welcoming Church movement is adding congregations to its list at a rapid rate. Resources for churches and individuals seeking to address gay/lesbian/bisexual concerns are being produced, and the visibility and strength of many denominational groups are on the upswing.

From my position within the United Church of Christ as a member on the coordinating council of the United Church Coalition for Lesbian/Gay Concerns (UCCL/GC), we cannot keep up with the requests, demands, and needs for our work and attention. A very significant step in our journey toward justice at this time is to build coalitions with other disempowered and oppressed groups and individuals. Realizing that our movement historically has been male-dominated and continues to be mostly Caucasian in membership, it is past time to deal more fully with our own racism, sexism, and classism if we truly seek to be the inclusive people of God.

Thus, it is important to note that the gay and lesbian movement within the church is a recent phenomenon, but not as recent as many may imagine. We have been there for decades—supporting, organizing, protecting, and seeking community. We have been present to one another and to the church. In many times and places we have created "church," when the institution has not welcomed us. We have prayed, marched, written letters, sung, studied, confronted, and celebrated. We have sought to be true to God and to ourselves.

The Welcoming Church Movement

The Welcoming Church movement has been described by many as one of the most exciting and enriching developments of the church in our lifetime. As reports of declining membership and finances seem to dominate the news about mainstream Protestant Christianity, something else is happening that is bringing new life, vitality, mission (and sometimes resources and members) to congregations across several denominations. Local churches are being empowered to claim the prophetic stance that God calls us to be inclusive communities, affirming the diversity of human sexual orientation, even if church law and/or tradition disapprove.

This journey, known ecumenically as the Welcoming Church movement, is growing quickly throughout rural, urban, and suburban congregations, large and small parishes, churches that historically have been on the forefront of social justice movements and churches that have not. Some of these churches have had a large percentage of "out" gay, lesbian, and bisexual persons before becoming Welcoming churches, although most have not. Some of these churches have lost members in the process, while many have gained members as a result of it. In other words, the Welcoming Church movement is, in itself, diverse—crossing denominational, cultural, and social boundaries. What unites these churches are the beliefs that gay/lesbian/bisexual persons are created in the image of God, just as heterosexual persons are, and that same-gender sexual expression and relationships are to be celebrated as sacred and loving. These churches affirm that the exclusion and oppression of gay/lesbian/bisexual persons by church and society is wrong, and declare themselves publicly to be inclusive and justice-seeking.

The process by which congregations become Welcoming may differ in some specifics according to denominational polity and practice; however, there are many similarities. Generally, each church must go through a study series focusing on homosexuality, homophobia, and religion, the starting point of which is usually the denomination's own Welcoming program curriculum/resources. These studies usually include sections concerning the experience of gay/lesbian/bisexual persons in church and society, biblical studies, theology, understanding homophobia and heterosexism, and the writing/reviewing of a Welcoming statement. Often, a study series will also include areas of specific interest to certain congregations. For example, a New Hampshire UCC congregation recently called me, seeking someone to do a presentation on the causes of homosexuality.

Churches will usually invite gay/lesbian/bisexual persons from within the congregation or elsewhere to tell their life stories. This may be the first time that some church members have heard a gay/lesbian/bisexual person speak about the painful effects of homophobia and the liberation of self-acceptance and love. Repeatedly, persons have told me that getting to know individuals and hearing their stories are the most moving aspects of the entire process. It is hard to condemn, ignore, or objectify someone you know. I have also heard many church members say that this was the first time in their church life that they felt challenged biblically and theologically and began to realize the impact of their assumptions. As one pastor told me, "My church members began to run home, dust off their Bibles, and really read them for a change!"

Upon completion of the study, the congregation is called to a vote. For some churches, this is a fairly smooth process and has a positive outcome. However, for others it is often more involved and demanding than originally anticipated. For example, I have known several churches that have engaged in the study a few times, as more and more members became interested and involved. I know other churches that have participated in the study but because of members' negative reactions have been unable to take it to a vote of the congregation.

In order to become an official part of the Welcoming Church movement, a church must take a vote. With this vote, a UCC congregation adopts an "Open and Affirming" (ONA) resolution, a United Methodist Church becomes a "Reconciling Congregation," a Lutheran church becomes "Reconciled in Christ," while a Presbyterian parish becomes a "More Light" church. Mennonite churches declare themselves "Supportive Congregations," American Baptists adopt statements as "Welcoming and Affirming Baptists," Disciples of Christ adopt "Open and Affirming" statements, and Unitarian Universalists proclaim themselves to be "Welcoming Congregations."

Once a congregation has publicly voted to become an official Welcoming Church, it then joins a large and growing denominational and ecumenical network. Each of the denominations listed above has a Welcoming Church program coordinator and resources/support specific to the denomination. For example, the United Methodist Reconciled in Christ program has held four national convocations, which have drawn persons from the United States, Canada, Australia, and England. The United

Church of Christ held its first ONA Exaltation in the fall of 1995, celebrating ten years of the ONA program. Often, denominational programs will offer newsletters and updates to its member churches. The Lutheran Church (ELCA) has a partners program in which congregations are asked to do local advocacy as well as provide support for Lutherans Concerned (the gay and lesbian advocacy/support group). In addition, the denominational program coordinators and others meet together to provide ecumenical support and resources. Perhaps the best known ecumenical resource is the quarterly magazine *Open Hands,* based in Chicago. Originally begun by the UMC's Reconciling Congregations program, it is now a publication of the UMC's Reconciled in Christ Program, the UCC's ONA program, the Lutherans' Reconciled in Christ Program, and the Presbyterians' More Light Churches Network. It is a superb magazine, in which each issue focuses on a specific area of concern within the church.

Once a church has declared itself to be Reconciled in Christ, Open and Affirming, Supportive, or Welcoming, some people believe that the hard part is over. However, this is far from true. As exciting, rejuvenating, and sometimes painful the process of studying and voting can be, some of the work begins only afterward. Specifically, the work of making gay/lesbian/bisexual persons feel welcomed and celebrated in church life is no easy task.

Often people imagine that once a vote is taken, suddenly hundreds of lesbian/gay/bisexual persons who have been standing outside will suddenly rush to knock down the church doors. The reality is quite different. (After all, we are dealing with generations of homophobic oppression, rooted in religious interpretations and beliefs.) Many gay/lesbian/bisexual persons have walked away from the church and are rightfully skeptical about anything positive the church may do or say. Therefore, in most cases, a church will have to reach out and communicate to lesbian/gay/bisexual folks that they are welcome and wanted and that, in fact, the congregation is repentant about the sins of homophobia and heterosexism. If one combines the publicity that the Christian right has received during the last few years with the historical and present stances of most mainstream denominations, it may be difficult for gay/lesbian/bisexual persons to believe that Christianity has anything healing or hopeful to offer. Thus, evangelism is a key tool of any Welcoming Church.

The most powerful evangelism in this case is probably the public work that the church can do to advocate and seek justice for lesbian/gay/bisexual persons in society. Churches and church members can put meaning into the words of any Welcoming Church statement by participating in pride marches, writing letters to the editor, organizing against antigay legislation, and speaking out wherever possible against homophobia and heterosexism.

In the 1995 New Hampshire pride march, Spirit of the Mountains sponsored an ecumenical worship service at the Capitol steps that included clergy from the United Church of Christ, the Episcopal Church, and the Unitarian-Universalist Association. The response was overwhelmingly positive, with many people coming to me afterwards, exclaiming how exciting it was for them to know that there are lesbian/gay/bisexual affirming ministers and churches in the area.

In addition to seeking publicity, outreach, and public advocacy, every church can take many more steps to become a more fully inclusive community. These involve including openly gay/lesbian/bisexual persons in church leadership roles, calling openly lesbian/gay/bisexual pastors, mentioning lesbian/gay/bisexual persons in both children's and adult's sermons and prayers, introducing hymns that include words such as *gay* and *lesbian,* and blessing same-gender relationships. Obviously, voting to declare one's church to be Open and Affirming, Reconciled in Christ, or the like does not end the process. Each denominational program has many ideas to help local parishes become more fully welcoming, many of which have come from other churches seeking to live out their call to be inclusive and just communities.

In 1978, the Welcoming Church movement first came into being as the More Light movement within the Presbyterian Church. Initiated by Presbyterians for Gay/Lesbian Concerns, this became a vehicle through which individual churches might dissent from the General Assembly's adoption of a minority report holding the traditional stance against gay and lesbian people. The phrase *more light* came from the majority report asking congregations to "seek more light" on the subject of homosexuality. As other denominational groups spawned similar programs, each adopted language and practices suitable to the particularities of its own denomination.

Although most programs are very similar, in that they ask churches (and sometimes other bodies within the denomination) to declare themselves to be welcoming or affirming of lesbian/gay/bisexual persons, there is one key difference, or difficulty, worth noting. First, most Welcoming Church programs are sponsored by caucuses and are in no way reflective of denominational polity or practices. In fact, they often conflict radically with denominational stances. For example, for a Presbyterian church to become a More Light church, it must be ready to face the consequences of breaking church law. Specifically, it is illegal for any parish to permit the full participation of openly lesbian or gay persons as members of governing councils, as deacons, or as elders. Thus, to vote to become a More Light church is to defy church law. In this and other denominations, churches run risks ranging from the loss of funds to expulsion from membership in the denomination. At this point, there are only two Welcoming Church programs with denominational sanction: the United Church of Christ and the Unitarian-Universalist Association. This is not to suggest that all members and congregations of these denominations are welcoming (far from it), but that denominational polity supports the full inclusion of lesbian/gay/bisexual persons in all aspects of church life, and has voted, through its governing body, the support for the ONA and Welcoming Congregations programs.

The United Church of Christ

Many persons in the United Church of Christ look to a few historic moments as key milestones in the journey toward justice for lesbian/gay/bisexual persons in the denomination. The first was the Golden Gate Association's 1972 ordination of Rev. Bill Johnson, the first openly gay or lesbian person to be ordained by a mainstream Christian church. Since that time, the number of openly gay/lesbian/bisexual persons being ordained to various calls within the church continues to increase steadily. Also, the number of clergy coming out within their parishes continues to rise as persons feel the need and find the capability to claim themselves as beloved children of God, called to serve God's people. At this point, the UCCL/GC is aware of about one hundred openly gay/lesbian/bisexual clergy throughout the denomination. This has not been achieved without significant struggle, pain, and loss on the part of many who have lost calls, been asked to leave churches, been refused recommendations for care by their congregations, or have simply not had their profile taken seriously because they are "out" on it.

In 1972, the UCC Gay Caucus (now the UCCL/GC and perhaps soon to be known by a more inclusive name) was founded by about thirty-five people. This group included—as it does today—gay, lesbian, bisexual, and heterosexual clergy and lay people. Although much is focused on issues of ordination and placement of openly gay/lesbian/bisexual clergy, the role and work of lay persons within local churches and at all levels of the denomination cannot be overstated. There are many openly gay/lesbian/bisexual lay people dedicated to the United Church of Christ and to sexual justice, who have taken great risks and have accomplished much in the work and life of local churches, the coalition, and the denomination.

During the first ten years of the UCCL/GC, much emphasis was placed on building a presence at General Synod, supporting gay and lesbian positive pronouncements and resolutions (see appendix B), and providing pastoral care and support to gay/lesbian/bisexual clergy, laity, and families. In 1981, the coalition's first national gathering was held in Rochester, N.Y., just prior to the thirteenth General Synod. National gatherings have been held every year since, and have become a lifeline for many. During General Synod years, there is much emphasis on organizing and preparation, while during the off years, there is more emphasis on program. Each gathering provides worship, support, networking, and solidarity with lesbian/gay/bisexual persons and our friends and families.

In 1983, at the fourteenth General Synod, the first ONA resolution was introduced, encouraging local churches to welcome gay and lesbian people. This resolution was debated and sent to the executive council for referral and study. Several months later, members of the Massachusetts UCCL/GC chapter revised the resolution and submitted it to the Massachusetts Conference annual meeting. It was adopted and then forwarded for consideration at the 1985 General Synod. In 1985, the fifteenth General Synod adopted the resolution, "Calling on United Church of Christ congregations to covenant as Open and Affirming." With this, the denominational ONA program was launched.

Since this time, the UCCL/GC has focused on a number of areas. As in the beginning, much effort continues to address the care and support of lesbian/gay/bisexual clergy and lay people throughout the denomination. Calls come in daily to the national office from gay/lesbian/bisexual persons seeking support, advice, and community. Our national gatherings have increased in size from thirty-five to over 150, and have shifted from including predominantly men to a more equal number of women and men. Regrettably, we are still predominantly white. We have launched a Youth and Young Adult (YYA) Ministries program, as well as providing leadership for the ONA program. We have published several helpful resources, including a same-sex blessing ceremonies packet, and we are working on liturgical resources for times of death and grieving. We continue to develop a network of conference chapters and seek to build coalitions with others working for justice. Essentially, we are growing fast and furiously, struggling to keep up with expanding needs and interests. At the 1995 national gathering, members voted to accept a five-year plan, in which we proposed the hiring of one full-time coordinator, increasing support for ONA and YYA, and consolidating our administration in order to expand our program. This requires major commitment, vision, and trust on the part of the coalition, and we hope that it will move us toward horizons in the coming years.

Once again, it is important to note that lesbian/gay/bisexual people have been in the church as long as there has been a church. Often we have been at the forefront of efforts to create justice and peace. Too often we have been working on behalf of others, and not nearly often enough as our own advocates. During the past twenty years, our efforts to name the injustices of church and society against us have led us to come out, come together, and proclaim that God's call to "bring release to the captives" includes us as much as anyone. Thus, in many denominations, support and advocacy groups, Welcoming Church programs, and many other steps toward our full and just inclusion have been growing with a spirit and vision unlike any other.

Questions for Discussion

1. How has your understanding of the gay/lesbian/bisexual movement within the church changed as a result of reading this chapter?

2. What new insights/information did you gain about gay/lesbian/bisexual persons within your own denomination? In other denominations?

3. How can you and your local church become more involved in the advocacy/support of gay/lesbian/bisexual persons within your denomination? ecumenically?

4. Is your church already a Welcoming Church? If so, how are you living out your covenant? What further steps do you need to take? If your church has not voted to become a part of the Welcoming Church movement, is now the time?

3...

The Body of Christ: Functional or Dysfunctional System?

There are numerous approaches, or lenses through which one might look, to observe and interpret the workings of the institutional church regarding any issue. Often, the dynamics and patterns of interaction are the same whether one is addressing becoming an Open and Affirming (ONA) congregation, changing the worship hour, or fixing the roof. Perhaps the exact aspect of church life one wishes to focus on determines the particular lens through which one looks. Specifically, one might view an area of interest through social psychology, philosophy, psychology, theology, history, or any one of several other approaches. Each lens presents a slightly different view of what one sees. Indeed, in regard to the concerns of gay/lesbian/ bisexual persons in church and society, all of these lenses represent valuable tools and perspectives for gaining insight and means of change.

Throughout years of my own study and reflection, I have come to believe that it is essential for us to understand some of the ways in which the church functions as a system. Knowing more about its structure of roles, relationships, and patterns of power and communication can help us understand why some things are so difficult to talk about and take so long to change. Thus, a family systems approach is a helpful lens through which one can begin to assess how the Christian church at large, and the United Church of Christ in particular, address and deal with the concerns of lesbian/gay/bisexual persons. It is also a way to gain an understanding of the homophobia and heterosexism interwoven into the structure and functions of church life.

For generations the Christian church has often been spoken of as "a family." Implicit in this metaphor is the assumption that many of the concerns, issues, roles, structures, joys, and problems of both biological and chosen families are also inherent in church life.

In addition to the perspective of family systems theory, object relations theory also provides significant insights into the role of homophobia and heterosexism and their psychological effects. Object relations theory offers another tool to understand the workings of homophobia and heterosexism within the individual as well as on a social or systemic level. Concepts such as splitting and projection help to explain more clearly why many church members cannot sit through a brief study session concerning homosexuality and be expected to change their deep and even unconscious feelings and reactions.

Given this experience and understanding of institutional church life, some of the theories within the family systems school of thought prove especially helpful. Particularly pertinent is the work of Salvador Minuchin in his development of structural family therapy. Within this theoretical framework, the interaction of the therapist him/herself with the family system provides the data and material for the assessment and understanding of the system, the situation, and the therapeutic goals and process. Minuchin writes, "Family structure is not an entity readily available to the observer. The therapist's data and his [or her] diagnosis are achieved experientially in the process of joining the family. He [or she] hears what the family members tell . . . but he [or she] also observes."[1]

If one replaces the word *family* in this quotation with the word *church,* and replaces the word *therapist* with *member* or *participant,* then one may conclude that the experience of lesbian, gay, bisexual, or heterosexual church members is a valid lens through which to focus. One's interactions with these persons and experiences are critical. In other words, being conscious of one's own experience of the institutional system is a valid entry point to gain insight.

This is a very significant point for congregations beginning to address the concerns of gay/lesbian/bisexuality within the church. I know that I have sat through countless discussions on homosexuality in national, conference, association, and local church settings, feeling completely invisible. Too often I have felt like the issue to be debated rather than the person to be met in relationship. It is dehumanizing and distancing to be discussed intellectually (or through the facade of intellectualism) in place of being listened personally. We are not engaged in a "value-free" debate here (assuming that such were possible). We are involved in the real-life justice-seeking struggles of people who have been silenced. Our experience, in and of itself, is a valid starting point to understanding what the church has done and needs to do. When heterosexual people ask me what they can do in this journey, my response is, *"Listen, listen, listen"* to the stories of gay/lesbian/bisexual persons. If you believe that you have no gay/lesbian/bisexual persons in your congregation, you are not making it safe for people to speak. If you believe that you have heard it all, because you have heard it once in a sermon or study session, you are not listening enough. Stop analyzing and start listening. We want to be heard.

The starting point of structural family therapy lies within the understanding that a family (or institution) is more that the individuals who make it up. As has been previously noted, "the whole is more than the sum of the parts." The family or institution is built on certain transactional patterns that become its structure, with rules that govern these transactions. These rules may or may not by explicitly stated, yet they are very powerful and significant. According to Minuchin, "These arrangements, though usually not explicitly stated or even recognized, form a whole—the structure of the family. The reality of the structure is of a different order from the reality of the individual members."[2]

Thus, it becomes critical to note that as valid as any one person's experience of the system is, it is not the entire experience, reality, or truth. This is crucial to understand, especially when addressing an issue of controversy within the church. Often in the life of the church, as in the life of a family, two individuals may experience something in ways that are radically different and are only a part of the whole. Yet in controversial matters, the "one" often presumes to have the truth for the "whole."

Perhaps the clearest example of this from my own experience in the United Church of Christ has to do not with sexuality but with our understanding of ourselves as a denomination. Several years ago when I was a student at Vanderbilt Divinity School, I was serving as an intern pastor at Brookmeade Congregational, United Church of Christ. One Sunday morning after the service, I was greeting people at the rear of the sanctuary. At this point, a visitor to the congregation introduced herself to me and told me that she was visiting from her home parish in New England. Then she said, "I don't know why all these people insist on saying UCC all the time . . . don't they know that we're Congregationalists?" A newcomer to the denomination myself, I became confused as the denominational motto ("that they may all be one") kept sounding in my head. I was clear that I had become part of the United Church of Christ, as my local church experience had confirmed with UCC hymnals and constant references to the UCC. The idea and the word "Congregationalism" never really seemed that significant. I could not understand why this woman said this with such feeling. A few years later, however, when I moved to Boston, I began to understand. The history and tradition of New England Congregationalism has such deep roots in the region that this was this woman's individual and communal church identity. In Nashville, Tennessee, and across the South, however, it is the United Church of Christ that is putting down roots. That is what had become my own, and this small parish's, denominational identity.

Both of us were right. Both of us were also wrong in that we were each limited in our experience and perspective. Even if both perspectives were combined, there would be only a limited truth and understanding of the larger reality, since neither of us had in our immediate consciousness any understanding or empathy for the Evangelical and Reformed tradition that is also part of the UCC.

In the arena of gay/lesbian/bisexuality within and across the United Church of Christ and all mainline Protestant denominations, numerous experiences, beliefs, and perspectives have emerged and seem to be coexisting in an often painful and tense unholy alliance. For example, one person's experience may be terribly painful and lead that person to believe that the UCC is a totally patriarchal, heterosexist institution beyond redemption. Another person's experience may be of the UCC as more inclusive and open than his or her former denomination, causing him or her to believe that the UCC is a progressive symbol of hope for Christianity. Still a third member may experience the UCC in a flux of change, especially in regard to issues of sexual justice. A fourth person may believe that the UCC is "headed by a bunch of heathens" (this is a direct quote from a conversation heard during coffee hour at one rural New Hampshire church). This person may believe that the UCC needs to seek forgiveness for its national policies.

In the understanding of systems theory, the reality of the structure of the institution is different from the reality of the individual. None of the aforementioned perspectives captures anything close to the whole truth or reality of the United Church of Christ as it addresses gay/lesbian/bisexual concerns, yet each is reality for someone.

One example of the ways in which this concept is helpful is to imagine the beginning of an Open and Affirming study series in a local church. As people begin any kind of challenging study, they are often quite defensive. Some will feel their position in the system to be threatened, and as a result, will become even more rigid in their assumption that *their* experience, truth, reality is *the* experience, truth, and reality for all. Pointing this out and affirming that everyone is bringing his/her history, needs, and feelings to this process can help to defuse some of the conflict. After all, some of this conflict has nothing to do with sexuality or theology, but with security and power in the system. Only through knowing and naming the diversity of experience can we begin to understand the whole. As the lyrics of the historical Congregational hymn based on the words of John Robinson (1620) state:

We limit not the truth of God to our poor reach of mind,
By notions of our day and sect,
Crude, partial, and confined.
No, let a new and better hope
Within our hearts be stirred:
O God, grant yet more light and truth
To break forth from
Your Word.[3]

The Principles of Family Systems Theory and the Church

Three of the basic principles on which family systems theory is founded help to provide insight into the workings of the church. These principles primarily come from the structural-strategic school of family therapy, specifically the work of Salvador Minuchin. They are:

1. The family is a system with parts in mutual interaction.
2. The key to the family is the position of its parts and their relationship to one another.
3. Who we know ourselves to be as individuals is greatly influenced by our interactions within the context of the system.[4]

1. The Family Is a System with Parts in Mutual Interaction

The family (or the church in this study) is not just an aggregate of various elements or individuals; rather, the system is a combination of relationships. Therefore, one cannot know the system by separately knowing its parts, for the whole is greater than the sum of the parts. Therefore, a change in one part or position of the system creates a change in another part or position. In trying to create change through this kind of therapy, the therapist does not focus on any one individual— even if the family members voice concerns about only one person. Instead, the therapist focuses on any and all individuals within the context of the family. As the family changes, each of the individuals changes accordingly. As Minuchin explains, "Therapy based on this framework is directed toward changing the organization of the family. When the structure of the family group is transformed, the positions of members in that group are altered accordingly. As a result, each individual's experience changes."[5]

This is a very important concept to address when one is concerned with the effects of homophobia in the church, and more particularly when one is seeking to create change in people's experience of homophobia and heterosexism. One cannot isolate one's experience of homophobia or presume to make changes in one person's or group's experience without creating change for everyone else in the system. This is true on all levels of the denomination, as each subsystem interacts with others, as well as being true with all individuals.

This is, I believe, an important key to understanding the process of conflict management within an organization such as the church. Specifically, when any issue or concern is "taken on" by any one subsystem or person within the system, then it will inevitably create change for the other subsystems and individuals as well. Change is uncomfortable and often resisted. Therefore, some of the conflict over issues, concepts, and concerns may be, in fact, conflict over the experience of change. Perhaps addressing the experience of change also can reduce the volatility of the issue.

One example of this process occurred in a small rural parish in which I served as pastor for several years. During an adult discussion series entitled "The Church and Homosexuality," one of the long-term members of the church began voicing his concerns about "too many homosexuals and people from out of town coming to the church." Through a lengthy discussion we determined that, in part, he was expressing his difficulty with the changes that had occurred during the past few years. The congregation had grown rapidly, to the point where people were wearing name tags and running out of refreshments during coffee hour. This man was grieving the loss of the small rural congregation in which all members had known one another intimately for generations. The experience of rapid change was at least as difficult as the issue at hand.

Similarly, when I was serving a large urban congregation, I had many conversations with an elderly white man who had been active in this church all his life. He repeatedly expressed his anger and distress over the church's emphasis on social justice issues. I vividly recall him crying out, "My church is changing!" with heartfelt pain. Again, he was reacting to his experience of change as much as or more than to the issues themselves.

On the other hand, I myself have felt, and have heard many others express the exact opposite feeling, crying out, "How long do we have to wait, patiently, calmly, feeling marginalized until they are comfortable with change?" Change is about power. Had the Israelites waited until the Egyptians were comfortable with change, we would still be slaves.

Like a family, the church is a system in which persons and groups engage in constant mutual interaction. To better understand this interactional principle, imagine a local UCC congregation in a small town in New England. No members of this congregation have ever discussed the topic of homosexuality in church. Seemingly out of nowhere, the congregation's three delegates to the conference annual meeting return to the church with Open and Affirming study packets; they talk energetically about the church's call to bring justice to lesbians and gay men and express the hope that this congregation will become one of the first Open and Affirming churches in the conference. Obviously, this change in one part of the system is going to create a change in other parts of the system. Closeted lesbians and gay men in the parish may be relieved or frightened. Parents who have ostracized their gay/lesbian children may be angry or sad. Parents who feel isolated and "closeted" in the support of their gay/lesbian children may feel supported. Possible reactions and changes are countless.

Another example of this interactional principle has recently occurred in the New Hampshire Conference, as well as across the denomination. In 1987, a chapter of the United Church Coalition for Lesbian/Gay Concerns (UCCL/GC, the denominational advocacy and support group for lesbian/gay/bisexual persons) was begun in the New Hampshire Conference. The next year, the conference annual meeting passed an Open and Affirming resolution. During this time, the support for lesbian/gay/bisexual persons was voiced as never before. At the same time, the Biblical Witness Fellowship—a organized group of UCC members who, among other things, considers homosexuality a sin from which people need to be healed—also grew in visibility and strength in the conference. The Biblical Witness Fellowship began to submit counterresolutions, to vocalize their opinions in workshops, and to hand out literature more fervently than in the past. This is an example of a change in the structure of the system creating a change in everyone's experience. A system exists with parts in mutual interaction so that one can only know it by understanding the experience of the whole, including these two subsystems, as well as the experience of others in the conference.

This principle is also strongly at work in the larger society. As more gay and lesbian people have stepped out of the closet, seeking civil rights and organizing for legal justice, there has been a kind of backlash.

As Irvashi Vaid observes, "As the American gay and lesbian movement approaches its sixth decade of political activism, it finds itself at a contradictory juncture. . . . [O]ur movement has been a staggering success . . . yet, gay and lesbian people remain profoundly stigmatized. . . . A backlash against gay rights swells at the same instant we witness the widest cultural opening gay people have ever experienced."[6]

The more visibility gay and lesbian people have, the more the antigay movement becomes organized. This is evidenced through such developments as the recent increase in antigay violence and increased legislation and legislative efforts to prevent civil rights from protecting gay and lesbian people. The National Gay and Lesbian Task Force can provide current information on these efforts.

2. The Key to the Family Is the Position of Its Parts and Their Relationship to One Another

The second foundational principle of systems theory is that the key to a system is the position of its parts and their relationship to one another. In other words, the parts of a system do not function according to their intrinsic nature alone, but according to their position within the system. In fact, the system is part of the intrinsic and ontological nature of any part within it. This is referred to as the "principle of symmetry," and can best be understood through the metaphors of either the human body or a basketball team. Each part or player functions differently as determined by its position in the system. A change in the position of one produces a change in the positions of the others.[7] The parts of any system function as a subsystem, and each system is part of a suprasystem. Each of these parts can be observed according to its own position in relation to the other parts of the system. One can easily see the connection between this psychosocial theory and basic Christian theology of the church as the body of Christ.

This assertion of systems theory is very helpful in trying to observe and understand the effects of homophobia and the experience of lesbian/gay/bisexual persons in the church. To observe the position of lesbian/gay/bisexual persons within the system of the church offers significant insight. For example, if lesbian/gay/bisexual persons openly function only in isolated subsystems, then their interaction and influence within the larger system are limited. However, if lesbian/gay/bisexual persons openly function in positions of authority and power in the system, then their influence will be greater. And finally, if lesbian/gay/bisexual persons function openly in various positions within the subsystems, system, and supra-system, then their influence and relationships extend much more broadly.

This particular principle of systems theory constitutes one of the most significant questions being asked by persons seeking to empower the United Church of Christ to become more Open and Affirming and bring justice to those who have experienced discrimination due to sexual orientation. The question is, Where in the system do openly lesbian/gay/bisexual persons and their advocates need to be in order to influence the system? Obviously, the greater the diversity of positions and the stronger the authority inherent in these positions, the greater the influence throughout the system—although, undoubtedly, this also will increase the experience of backlash and the ensuing rigidity of heterosexist boundaries. Therefore, this constitutes a problem in creating systemic change. Specifically, as lesbian/gay/bisexual persons come out, we often find our authority questioned or removed by the community at large and are forced to relinquish our positions and/or influence within the larger system, often regrouping with a supportive subsystem.

Certainly, more openly gay/lesbian/bisexual persons hold leadership positions in the clergy and laity today than did ten years ago; however, this alone does not guarantee real or long-lasting systemic change. At this point, a little under 3 percent of United Church of Christ congregations have declared themselves Open and Affirming; and, in reality, even these churches could reverse their stance through a congregational vote.

The place of lesbian/gay/bisexual persons and our concerns within the denominational structure is now a critical issue. In local church communities, lesbian/gay/bisexual persons and their parents and friends are coming out in their positions as active members. I cannot recall how many times I have heard people say that "once the issue has a face," it can never be thought of in the same way.

There are also numerous gay/lesbian/bisexual clergy seeking calls as parish pastors. However, in reality, most of these ministers are closeted and well aware that coming out will involve at least a very long and painful search process and may mean being denied the call or forced to resign. In other denominations, coming out means the instant revocation of ordained status and call as stated by denominational polity. ("Coming out" means, in this context, that the minister has informed the congregation of his/her sexual orientation without asking anyone to maintain silence or secrecy.) At this point there are between thirty and thirty-five openly gay/lesbian/bisexual pastors serving parishes across the entire denomination. These are in addition to the few who are involved in the creation of potential new congregations focusing on the specific pastoral and liturgical needs of the lesbian/gay/bisexual community. However, many more gay/lesbian/bisexual clergy have come out and, for a variety of reasons, are no longer serving parishes; and many more are coming out on profiles and being called to positions. In 1994, an openly gay couple, Peter Ilgenfritz and Dave Schull, were called as co-associate pastors of the University Christian Church in Seattle, Washington. However, they were called only after two years of searching and over one hundred rejections.

The members of the UCCL/GC are trying constantly to advocate for the position of gay/lesbian/bisexual persons throughout the denomination. Specifically these efforts include fostering a strong and visible presence at General Synod meetings, nominating openly lesbian/gay/bisexual persons to various councils and boards, and raising the concerns of lesbian/gay/bisexual persons on all levels of the denomination, as well as providing resources for ministry with gay/lesbian/bisexual youth and young adults, and supporting the Open and Affirming movement.

Finally, in the midst of these efforts to broaden and deepen the positions and influence of the concerns of lesbian/gay/bisexual persons throughout the system, there is a simultaneous move toward increasing the strength of various subsystems that address these concerns and needs. The UCCL/GC continues to provide a subsystem of ongoing support and networking in order to decrease the isolation experienced by lesbian/gay/bisexual persons. This support is offered through a regular newsletter, annual gatherings, and the fostering of regional and national networks of relationships. Many in the larger system are probably not even aware that this subsystem exists, let alone its importance in the lives of so many.

In addition to this subsystem, there are approximately four to five new church starts and/or organized congregations presently emerging as grassroots efforts to provide church community for lesbian/gay/bisexual persons and for heterosexual persons who wish to worship within a community grounded in sexual justice. These congregations exist in places as diverse as Cleveland, Minneapolis, and Concord, New Hampshire. It is hoped that the emergence of these congregations provides a safe church home for those who have felt excluded by traditional parishes, and at the same time signals to the larger church the importance and strength of ministry with, by, and on behalf of lesbian/gay/bisexual persons in the United Church of Christ.

Each of these subsystems as well as the system itself are a part of and are influenced by two very significant larger systems: specifically, the ecumenical church and the surrounding culture/society. Other churches' work on the issues of ordaining lesbian/gay/bisexual persons influences the work of the UCC, and vice versa. At this point, the UCC and the Unitarian-Universalist Church are the only Christian denominations to vote in their national legislative bodies for the ordination of noncelibate lesbian/gay/bisexual persons.

Thus, it could be stated that within the larger system of the ecumenical Christian church, the UCC is the most supportive and progressive denomination. However, because of the structure of Congregationalism, clergy and lay members continue to experience significant oppression and ostracism on local and conference levels. In other words, no matter how many pronouncements and resolutions about sexual justice are issued on a national level, the local church is empowered to hire and fire the clergy it wants. Therefore, if a local church chooses to continue in heterosexist traditions and patterns, there is very little the denominational leadership can do about it.

I hear about people's dissonant experience of the UCC on a regular basis. For example, I recently officiated at a lesbian covenanting ceremony which persons from several states in New England and the Midwest attended. After the service, one gay man asked in what denomination I had been ordained and was serving. When I responded, "The UCC," he said, "The UCC? That's my church. I was raised in that church. I can't imagine that my church ordained you. This is great, but I still can't quite believe it!"

In the summer of 1995, I spoke with one of the lesbian participants in the UCCL/GC national gathering. She told me her story about how she had first come to a national gathering several years ago at the urging of a friend. She found it to be one of the most spiritually empowering and healing moments of her life. Thus, upon her return home, she tried searching for a local church to join, even though she had not been to church for years (that is, not since she had come out as a lesbian). She described visiting several congregations and feeling silenced, invisible, and unwelcome. Her pain and shock were evident as she described having these two radically different experiences of the United Church of Christ. Thus, she now says that the UCCL/GC national gathering is "her church," and she has given up the search for a local congregation. Although the UCCL/GC national gatherings can be profoundly spiritual communities, they cannot take the place of local church involvement. After all, they only happen once a year. Therefore, both this woman and the local churches in her area are missing out on spiritual communion and community.

Another dynamic similar to this concerns the local parish. Specifically, churches may find that the input and pressure from the surrounding homophobic secular culture are so strong and pervasive that they override the input from the national church. This is often the experience of small rural churches in New Hampshire and in other regions, which exist within a conservative political and social environment. Often the culture and mores of the local town feel much closer and more significant than that of the national church. Thus, the suprasystem, the system, and various subsystems each have a different experience of the same reality. It might be said that each has a part or perspective of the reality, and that each of these parts, perspectives, and experiences may be very different from one another.

3. Who We Know Ourselves to Be as Individuals Is Influenced by Our Interactions within the System

The third foundational point of systems theory states that our experience of who we are as individuals—in our minds, our spirits, our selves—is greatly influenced by our interactions within the context of the system. The point here is that our inner psychic and spiritual life is not entirely our own, nor is it self-contained. Minuchin places this axiom of structural family therapy within the context of the sociological and anthropological thought of the later twentieth century. He contrasts this to traditional psychodynamic theory with its emphasis on the individual.

> Individual psychodynamic thinking drew upon a different concept, that of [the human being] as a hero, remaining him[/her]self in spite of circumstances. . . . This perception of the individual could survive in a world where the resources of [humankind] seemed infinite. . . . Modern technology has changed this view. . . . As early as 1914, Ortega y Gasset wrote: "I am myself plus my circumstances. . . . The most recent biological science studies the living organism as a unit composed of the body and its particular environment so that the life process consists not only of the adaptation of the body to its environment, but also of the adaptation of the environment to the body. The hand tries to adjust itself to the material object in order to grasp it firmly; but at the same time, each material object conceals a previous affinity with a particular hand."[8]

In other words, one cannot know oneself separate from one's exchanges and interactions with one's environment. There is no concept of the self that does not include these interactions.

This is perhaps easy to understand in relation to persons within the church as they come to terms with sexuality in general and homosexuality in particular. For example, if one is raised within an Open and Affirming congregation and/or a congregation that has an active openly lesbian/gay/bisexual membership, then one's attitude about homosexuality and religion is probably going to be very different from someone raised in a congregation in which gay/lesbian/bisexual concerns are silenced or in which lesbians and gay men are prayed for as sinners in need of reorientation. Anyone's inner psychic life would be significantly affected by such experiences; however, a lesbian/gay/bisexual person growing up would have an entirely different sense of self and self-worth given the different context.

Two members of the clergy, who were interviewed for this project, provide clear examples of this point—that who we know ourselves to be is greatly influenced by our environment.

One described being raised as a child in a congregation in which there were active lesbian and gay members. In fact, she recalls the importance of having had an openly lesbian church school teacher as an adolescent. This clergywoman states that she never struggled to accept herself as a lesbian; instead, she simply knew that about herself in the same way that she came to know other parts of herself through growing up. After being ordained and searching for a church, she describes being shocked at the homophobia in congregations and feeling unprepared to deal with it. Nevertheless, she states that she never doubted herself or her value as a human being, because she continues to remember the feedback from her first pastors and church community. In addition, she remains in communication with them, and therefore, continues to receive positive feedback about herself and about her sexual orientation as one part of who she is.

On the other hand, another member of the clergy recounts having heard repeatedly as a child, at home and in church, about the "moral depravity of homosexuals," along with gay-bashing jokes and other homophobic and heterosexist comments. He recalls his deep inner struggle to accept himself as a gay man, and has spent years worried about the effects of his family or church discovering his homosexuality. He talks about his decision to transfer from his home denomination to the UCC because he had seen "too many of my gay brothers commit suicide, and I don't want that to happen to me." This man has struggled painfully and often silently, because he has known himself to be "bad, sinful, and sick" from the feedback of his childhood church and home. One's sense of self cannot be isolated from the interactions and exchanges within one's environment.

Family Systems Theory and Sexual Orientation in the Church

My personal experience as a lesbian Christian has been one of seeking to remain active in my Christian faith without sacrificing my sense of self worth-and self-esteem. Through my personal experience and my professional experience as a pastor for more than ten years, I have come to believe that the "dysfunctional," alcoholic, or pathological family system is a profoundly appropriate model for understanding the church's dealing with homophobia and homosexuality. A major component of these dysfunctional systems is keeping secrets in order to avoid conflict. The work of family therapists in the area of secret-keeping is helpful in trying to understand some of the ways in which homophobia and heterosexism are reinforced in the church.

In *It Will Never Happen to Me: Children of Alcoholics,* Claudia Black describes the three rules of alcoholic family systems: "Don't talk, don't trust, don't feel."[9] Essentially, if one breaks these rules, or patterns of interaction and exchange, then one runs the risk of undermining the system organized around protecting the alcoholic. The rules prevent the real issue of alcoholism and its effects on members of the family from being acknowledged or discussed. Concerning the effects of secret-keeping on family systems, Black writes "helplessness despair, and hopelessness cause family members to believe—if you just ignore it, maybe it will go away."[10]

Carl Whitaker, another influential family systems therapist, acknowledges the particular impact of keeping family secrets. Whitaker frames this collusion of keeping secrets in the dynamic of family guilt. Essentially, he asserts that anytime a family member challenges the family's equilibrium (that is, its attitudes, myths, behaviors, etc.), then he or she will experience guilt, because we all internalize prohibitions against disturbing the family's equilibrium. This family guilt is not moral guilt, for revealing a family secret is not morally wrong (and, in the case of abuse, it is morally right). However, it often feels morally wrong because of the power of the internalized admonitions. Often, says Whitaker, we assume that if we raise a family member's anxiety and he or she complains, then we feel guilty. Yet, in telling the secret, we did not hurt the person, we simply raised his or her anxiety.[11]

The role of keeping secrets within a dysfunctional family system is similar to the role and effects of keeping secrets in the church system. First, the church sometimes exhibits many of the characteristics described of dysfunctional or alcoholic family systems. In one sense, the reality of gay/lesbian/bisexual persons in the church has been like the proverbial "elephant in the living room" of the dysfunctional family: Everyone in the family knows that the elephant is there, and in fact has to maneuver around it quite regularly as it blocks both vision and access to one another, but no one ever talks about it. Nor does one allow oneself to feel upset by this elephant, because everyone knows that no one will ever deal with it anyway.

Gay/lesbian/bisexual persons have been active in all levels of participation and leadership of the church throughout all time. However, the message has been clear: *"Don't talk about it!"*

Second, there is a striking parallel between the anxiety of telling family secrets and telling the truth about gay/lesbian/bisexual persons within the church. A message is projected onto the lesbian/gay/bisexual person that to tell the truth would somehow upset the system and raise too much conflict, preventing the congregation from doing its "real work."

This was recently brought home to me through a very painful reminder in my work with Spirit of the Mountains. When a gay man who had been one of our most active participants died, his parents tried not to acknowledge his homosexuality and asked their minister to officiate at the memorial service. When I spoke with the minister the next day about the ethics of this, he responded by saying that it would not be helpful to raise any conflict at this point. Thus, the needs of the gay/lesbian/bisexual community once again were set aside in order to "keep peace" in the system.

The lesbian/gay/bisexual person in turn, internalizes this message of silence, and experiences church/family guilt for raising anxiety in the system. Within the church, this can be all-too-easily misidentified as moral guilt or sin. Then, the experience of telling the truth can cause someone to feel shamed for disturbing the people of God rather than liberated in the truth that makes us free.

I recall a vivid reminder of this rule and the pathology of family/church guilt in my own personal journey of sexuality and spirituality. One Sunday afternoon in 1980, I was sitting with my father on the back porch of my parents' home. I told him that I was going to return to an old dream I had from a long time ago. I had decided to leave social work school and enter seminary. His only response on that day (although his response has changed since) was, "You have a problem—it won't work." He did not have to say more, since he was uncomfortable with saying the words and I knew exactly what he meant. What he was saying without saying it directly was that lesbians do not "make it" in the church if we tell anybody who we really are, or perhaps even if we don't tell.

In many ways, my own experience has proven him correct. When I enrolled in theological school in 1979, I changed denominations. There are many reasons I chose the United Church of Christ in addition to its stand on sexual orientation. However, I knew that had I remained a United Methodist, there would have been no possibility for me to be ordained and/or serve as an open lesbian. It was painful to leave the church of my family and ancestors, but I knew it was necessary to pursue my vocation . I also knew that no matter what denomination I served in, once I came out publicly, it would be difficult to continue in most parish settings. Again, my father was right. Before coming out, I had served for three years in a very successful parish pastorate (and two years prior to that in a large urban congregation). Upon my coming out, such conflict emerged that the following three years were extremely difficult. It often felt as if the homophobic backlash prevented me from continuing the ministry to which I had been called, and instead required me to focus on the reactions to my lesbianism. Finally, I resigned, knowing that there had been both truth and concern in my father's words twelve years earlier.

The rules of family dysfunction raise another significant issue for lesbian/gay/bisexual persons within the church. This dilemma is known in family systems theory as the "double-bind." One experiences a double-bind when one is caught in conflicting messages from the system. Nichols defines the double-bind as "A conflict created when a person receives contradictory messages on different levels of abstraction in an important relationship, and cannot leave or comment."[12]

Lesbian/gay/bisexual persons experience this double-bind when the church exclaims through its preaching that we are all beloved children of God just as we are, but then denies the ordination of lesbian/gay/bisexual persons. Another example of the double-bind occurs when the national polity of the denomination declares that sexual orientation is not a concern of ordination, and that gay/lesbian/bisexual persons are called to ministry just as are heterosexual persons, but then openly lesbian/gay/bisexual candidates are refused ordination by their association and cannot find a church that will call them. To leave or comment on these situations immediately places the relationship at risk.

Some persons might suggest that some of these "dysfunctional family rules" are changing, and in some places I would agree that they are. However, in many cases, these changes are reluctant responses from one subsystem to the action of another subsystem, as well as responses to the larger system of society as it addresses questions of gay/lesbian/bisexual civil rights.

Within the approach of structural family systems theory, Minuchin summarizes pathology as a family's inability to face demands for change. These demands for change emerge from various biopsychosocial developments within individuals, subsystems, and the larger suprasystem in which all members are imbedded. Pathology develops when the system cannot change or adjust its responses to these external and internal demands for change.

> A dysfunctional family is a system that has responded to these internal or external demands for change by stereotyping its functioning. . . . The accustomed transactional patterns have been preserved to the point of rigidity, which blocks any possibility of alternatives. Selecting one person to be the problem is a simple method of maintaining a rigid, inadequate family structure.[13]

An example of this kind of rigidity of response occurred at a 1994 legislative hearing in New Hampshire on House Bill 1432,

which would have added "sexual orientation" to the antidiscrimination laws. A minister went to the microphone and began
to read scripture. He refused to stop when his time was up, and
was interrupted only when officials turned off the microphone
and escorted him away. At the same hearing, an example of
"selecting one person to be the problem" occurred repeatedly
when a few persons blamed homosexuals for everything from
the demise of "the family," to economic problems, to the present
health care crisis. These responses to the demand for change are
rigid and inadequate. Again, such responses are occurring with
greater frequency as lesbian/gay/bisexual persons come out of
the closet, speak out, and organize for basic legal protection
across the country.

Given this understanding of dysfunction, Minuchin offers
three reasons why persons change: "First, they are challenged in
their perception of their reality. Second, they are given alternative possibilities that make sense to them. And third, once they
have tried out the alternative transactional patterns, new relationships appear that are self-reinforcing."[14]

I have witnessed many persons within the church change
their opinions and beliefs about lesbian/gay/bisexual persons. I
remember one man in particular, a member of the church I
served when I came out as a lesbian. Since he knew me as a pastor before he knew me as a lesbian, he stated that he had
changed his feelings about lesbian/gay/bisexual ministers and
was "proud" to have a lesbian pastor. However, he also said that
he would not feel as comfortable with a gay man for his pastor.
During the following year, he met several gay men, some of
whom were clergy. At one point, I reminded him of his statement about gay men and asked him if he still felt the same. He
laughed and said, "I can't believe I used to think that way."

According to Minuchin's theory, this man was challenged in
his perception of reality. Second, he was presented with alternative possibilities. And finally, these new possibilities developed into relationships that were self-reinforcing. This is how
change happens. The key here is not to make lesbian/gay/bi-
sexual persons responsible for the change. Appropriate inter-

ventions must occur that support the changed relationships. These interventions can range from economic support of out pastors to dialogues between lesbian/gay/bisexual community leaders and church leaders. Essentially, the kind and degree of interventions are limited only by our creativity.

As has been stated throughout this chapter, the contributions of structural family therapy and the work of Salvador Minuchin are very helpful in providing a lens through which to view the role of homophobia/heterosexism and the experience of lesbian/gay/bisexual persons in the church. However, this lens has its limitations which need to be acknowledged and enhanced with additional perspectives.

In *The Family Interpreted,* Deborah Anna Luepnitz criticizes the limits of structural family therapy because of its dependence on the concepts of functionalism. Essentially, functionalism explains how the parts of a system fit together but has difficulty explaining why or how they can be fundamentally at odds with one another. In the logic of functionalism, if something occurs, it must be filling a social need for all parties involved. Luepnitz explains, "Functionalist explanations can justify almost anything in terms of some punitive social need. Functionalist historians have even argued that lynchings and witch hunts serve a social need, i.e., a cathartic or 'therapeutic' need. Therapeutic for whom? one might well ask."[15]

In other words, use of the organismic model of society which underscores functionalism and structuralism may well be able to describe how something works but not to evaluate why it works or for whom it works. Nor can it discern for whom it does not work or whom it sacrifices. Because of its emphasis on the system, structural family therapy can overfocus on the maintenance of the system at the expense of the individual.

Therefore, in terms of the relationship between gay/lesbian/ bisexual persons and the church, it is not only important to talk of mutual exchange, patterns of interaction, change, conflict, and positions. It is also critical to raise questions of how these have developed, whom they serve, and whom they hurt or alienate. In order to answer these questions, one must look at the historical development of the system and the effects of intergenerational cycles.

In his work with the families of schizophrenics, Murray Bowen developed the concept of the "multigenerational transmission process," which "defines the principle of projection of varying degrees of immaturity (undifferentiation) to different children when the process is repeated over a number of generations. . . . [It] provides a base from which to make predictions in the present generations and gives an overview of what to expect in coming generations."[16]

This is related to Bowen's concept of the "family projection process." In this process, Bowen asserts that the parents transmit anxiety to the children so that children end up with about the same level of differentiation as the preceding generation. Differentiation in this theory is described as the lifelong process of being in balance between self and others, and being able to be as clear as possible about one's values, beliefs, and decisions. It is also described as the level of fusion with the system. The higher the level of differentiation, the lower the fusion and the stronger the "solid self." Conversely, lower differentiation creates a stronger "pseudo-self" and propensity to high fusion.[17] These concepts point out some significant factors in the role of homophobia in the church and the effects on lesbian/gay/bisexual persons.

If the values of preceding generations have been rooted in a patriarchal cultural and religious world view, it will affect the position of lesbian/gay/bisexual persons today. Patriarchy is the enforced belief in male dominance and control while sexism is the system that keeps women subordinate to men.[18] This ideological system is fundamentally antithetical to the liberation of women, persons of color, lesbian/gay/bisexual persons, and others who do not fit the patriarchal mold. (For more on this, see chapter 1 concerning homophobia and heterosexism.) To threaten these values is to threaten the system that upholds them; therefore, anxiety about sexual diversity and liberation will be passed down from one generation to the next. One can see the power of this legacy through catchphrases such as "traditional family values." Depending on a generation's or an individual's level of differentiation, persons may or may not be able to contain this anxiety appropriately and make changes that are liberating.

As a system, the church has transmitted generations of anxiety about sex and sexuality, diversity of affectional and sexual expression, and gender roles. To tell the "family secret" of the cost of heterosexism and homophobia to the institution and the individuals within it will raise significant family guilt, which has been transmitted through the generations. In order to create positive changes psychologically, institutionally, and theologically, we must be willing to address and manage significant anxiety and guilt. Therefore, to take a unigenerational view of the role of homophobia/heterosexism is limited and naive and must be balanced with historical and social analysis.

Through these concepts, one can see that family systems theory offers some extremely helpful tools with which to address the issues of homophobia/heterosexism within the church today. An understanding of mutual exchange and feedback, organismic/environmental interdependence, the interactional principle, roles, and positions within the system is critical to bringing about any real change. However, the inquiry cannot begin and end with a unigenerational view. Instead, it must be expanded with such concepts as family guilt and intergenerational anxiety if one is to understand the real power of homophobia and its effects on gay/lesbian/bisexual and heterosexual persons in the church.

The Principles of Object Relations Theory and the Church

As was stated in the beginning of this chapter, the concepts of object relations theory also enhance this systemic understanding of the church's struggle with homophobia and homosexuality. It is my belief that several dynamics described in object relations theory take place on a systemic level as well as on an individual basis. In addition, many of the concepts of object relations theory have profound psychological implications for gay/lesbian/bisexual persons. Although many of these concepts have been interwoven throughout this chapter, it is important to lift up some of them for further consideration in order to understand their unique contributions to this study.

The basic premise of object relations theory is that the most profound motivator and need of being human is that of being in relation. This challenges Freudian psychology, which asserts that humans are primarily motivated by libidinal and aggressive drives. Psychoanalytic theory states that first and foremost we seek pleasure—that is, we seek to end the stress of our unmet drives. Essentially, everything serves this purpose. On the other hand, object relations theory states that being in relationship is not a means to an end but is the end, in and of itself. We are propelled by a fundamental need to be in relation from the beginning.

Even without the other concepts of object relations theory, this premise has profound implications for lesbian/gay/bisexual persons in the church. It suggests a conflict at the very core of what it is to be human. If our fundamental need is for relation, then the lesbian/gay/bisexual Christian within a homophobic institution is forced to choose between relationships and, therefore, will be left with core religious and psychological loss. Does one choose relationship with his or her intimate partner to the exclusion of relationship with the church, or does one choose relationship with the church to the exclusion of the intimate partner? In addition, if our fundamental need as humans is for relationship, and the church declares either overtly or covertly that the manifestation of this need is sinful, then lesbian/gay/bisexual persons are left confused, shamed, and frustrated in our core selves as created children of God. This is another way of understanding the double-bind presented earlier.

This leads to some of the basic concepts of object relations as they inform us in our understanding of the struggle of lesbian/gay/bisexual persons in the church. These concepts are splitting, projection, projective identification, and the internalization of shame.

Splitting

The concept of splitting was initially identified by Madeline Klein as a description of the process of pre-oedipal development. At this stage of life, the infant is entirely dependent on the mother as the primary caretaker. Due to a number of factors, mostly that of socialization, the relationship with the father is usually less significant in this stage. When the mother cannot constantly meet the needs of the infant, the child engages in the psychological act of splitting. Essentially, the child splits the mother into benevolent (good) components and destructive (bad) components, and then engages in a process of internalizing these good and bad objects in an inner world. This splitting into good and bad has a profound effect on our sense of self and our ability to relate to others throughout our lives. Sheldon Cashdan explains that "the dichotomy of goodness-badness not only constitutes a powerful and pervasive split in interpersonal functioning but also creates a deep pervasive split in interpersonal consciousness. The way that this split manifests itself in the course of maturation depicts the child's movement from extreme dependence to psychological autonomy."[19]

Again, this kind of psychological understanding is helpful in assessing the situation of lesbian/gay/bisexual persons in the church. The psychological split into good and bad can easily collude with the theological split of dualism. In a dualistic theological construct, everything is divided into good/bad, heaven/earth, spirit/body, spirituality/sexuality, male/female, heterosexual/homosexual. Inevitably, the gay/lesbian/bisexual person becomes aligned with the "bad" object, which is somehow juxtaposed to all that which is theologically and psychologically "good." The act of aligning and being aligned with bad, earth, body, sexuality, etc., contributes to the experience of isolation both socially and individually. In other words, persons who fit this half of the dualistic equation, for whatever reason, find themselves outside of relationship with the larger community (i.e., outside of the gate to the holy city), and relationships become polarized rather than integrated. This sense of dualism and polarization is held in place by a complex web of psychological and theological constructs, which are in turn lived out within the system of the church. It is no accident that in some traditions people speak of the "Mother Church," consciously and unconsciously proclaiming the psychological and theological power of the institution and their relationship with it.

The term *object* is a way of speaking of the internal representation of external persons. Kohut describes this through the term *selfobjects,* which refers to distinct, objectively separate individuals who eventually become incorporated into the self. These selfobjects are taken into the child and function to elicit feelings such as pride or guilt. Much of our experience of feelings such as greed, guilt, pride, and envy are functions of this process of internalization. There are numerous examples of this internalization in the experience of lesbian/gay/bisexual persons. Perhaps the comparison of the two clergy members referred to previously in this chapter is one of the clearest examples of this process. One minister internalized positive selfobjects through individuals (pastors, Sunday school teachers) and a community that affirmed her for her true self. The other minister, on the other hand, internalized negative selfobjects (family members, church leaders) who condemned his sexual urges and affectional attractions, creating significant internalized guilt and shame. Much of the process of accepting oneself as lesbian/gay/bisexual within a homophobic church and society is the process of naming the internalized selfobjects that have been condemning and shaming, so that one may begin to externalize them in order to create a healthy sense of self.

Projection

In addition to being internalized, these objects are also projected onto others. Each of us unconsciously projects part ego and part object into our relationships with others. This projection is not necessarily bad or good, but it simply is a part of our relational makeup. Without some level of projection, we would not be able to experience empathy or intimacy. However, when projections remain completely unconscious, then the projector can believe that he or she has an objective, rational, and full interpretation of the other, when in fact, he or she may only have what has been projected.

Again, this has profound implications for the relationship of gay/lesbian/bisexual persons with the church. Prior to my coming out, I would frequently ask church members if they knew any gay or lesbian persons. Often people would say no. (Since I was not out at the time, then they either were not aware or were upholding the conspiracy of silence.) When asked how they would know if someone were gay or lesbian, the response was often a list of stereotypical characteristics that frequently have nothing to do with the reality of gay/lesbian/bisexual people. Regularly, within the church and society, persons have projected the bad object onto the gay/lesbian/bisexual person through stereotyping and scapegoating, and have based their decisions about everything from civil rights to ordination on these projections.

This is another area in which Mel White's recent book, *Stranger at the Gate,* is extremely informative. He writes about this process of projection as one who had been on the "inside" of the religious right for many years, and is now on the "outside."

> Theirs (the religious right) is the politics of blame. Certain groups of "sinners" (gays and lesbians, for example) are being singled out as scapegoats for the nation's ills. Unless these "sinners" are purged, or so reason leaders of the radical right, America will be destroyed like Rome or Greece. . . . The trick, of course, is in determining who is the sinner and who is not. . . . To be successful at the politics of blame, one needs to single out the unholy other as a target and a scapegoat. The radical right has decided that others are to blame for the breakdown of the American family, for crime in the streets, for violence and illiteracy in the classroom, for hunger, poverty, and unemployment, for inadequate housing and health care. These Christian fundamentalists have not yet discovered that they, too, are a part of the problem.[20]

Projective Identification

The processes of splitting and projection lead to another important concept of object relations theory, projective identification, which describes a further step in the process of interpersonal interactions. Projective identification requires both the projector (the sender) of the object and the projectee (the target) of the projected object. Essentially, the recipient of the projection gets hooked into the message of the projector, so that he or she becomes pressured to think, feel, and behave in ways that are congruent with the projector's fantasies.

> In object relations theory, projective identifications are patterns of interpersonal behavior in which a person induces others to behave or respond in a circumscribed fashion. This differs from ordinary projection, which is essentially a mental act and need not involve overt responses of any sort. In the projection of hostility, for example, the person who projects assumes that people are angry or ill-tempered regardless of how they actually may feel or behave, What is more, there need not be any face-to-face interaction for the projection to occur. Projective identification, on the other hand, actually involves the behavioral and emotional manipulation of others.[21]

Again, this has profound implication for lesbian/gay/bisexual persons in the church. Perhaps the clearest example of the process occurred several years ago in a church I served. A lesbian couple who were both active members of the congregation asked me to perform their covenant service in the sanctuary of the church. They both wanted me as their pastor to lead the service, and they wanted it held in their church. Just as I did when heterosexual couples requested to be married, I raised the issue with the deacons. However, unlike any heterosexual request I had brought to them, they denied this one. The diaconate stated that although these women were liked by the congregation and were active members, there were too many other members who would be upset by this "blatant support" of a lesbian relationship. The projected message here was "You can be a part of us as long as you don't talk about your relationship or expect us to support who you are as a couple." This was a projection of shame, devaluing, and degradation of the relationship and isolation from the community. A few months later, the couple broke up without investing much time, effort, or emotionality in staying together. Subsequently, they also left the church. I believe that they, like many lesbian and gay couples, got caught up in the projection that same-gender relationships are not "real" relationships and, therefore, should not be expected to last. In the process of getting "caught" in the projection, they began to act the part, portraying a relationship that was as unstable and undervalued as others' projections onto it.

The Internalization of Shame

Another common projective identification that occurs within the system of the church involving lesbian/gay/bisexual persons is that of the projection and internalization of shame. As we have noted previously, the church and individuals within it often project sexual shame onto gay/lesbian/bisexual persons. As these persons are scapegoated and carry the burden of shame for the institution, the pathological splitting between good and bad continues with little hope for integration. In my pastoral counseling work, far too many lesbian/gay/bisexual persons have told me that they are just too ashamed to go back to church and that they cannot tolerate what other people believe about them, because they then begin to believe it about themselves.

> Two contradictory attitudes concerning lesbian sexuality prevail currently. One celebrates lesbian sexuality as being highly physically and emotionally gratifying; the second holds that low sexual desire is often a problem in lesbian relationships. . . . These two attitudes can be viewed as reflecting issues of sexual pride and shame, respectively, in lesbian relationships. Sexual pride results from a combination of feelings of joy and expressions of personal adequacy (Nathanson 1987). In contrast, sexual shame underlies many of the psychological factors believed to inhibit desire, including intrapsychic conflicts, internalized homophobia, fear of failure, and responses to traumatic sexual experiences. . . . Shame . . . occurs when perceived defects in the self are exposed.[22]

Internalized shame has profound significance in one's sense of self, psychologically and theologically. How can we have a healthy sense of ourselves as unique and beloved individual children of God if we are internalizing messages of shame in regard to our capacity for love and relationship?

As was stated in the beginning of this section, the concepts of object relations are valid intrapsychically and interpsychically—that is, individually and systemically. One perspective of object relations theory focuses not on the child, but on the adult process of codifying messages about the self in society. George Herbert Mead, a sociologist, states his sense that the process begun in childhood continues throughout adult life.

> The individual self is the mechanism by which society becomes incorporated into the human psyche. Because the self is constructed out of relationships with others and therefore involves the internalization of societal codes and conventions, it can be considered a miniature society within the individual. Just as the broader society guides the behavior of its institutions, so the inner miniature society guides the behavior of the individual.[23]

Again, this confirms the principles of systems theory in that we cannot be who we are in isolation. Instead, we are who we are because of the surrounding system.

Every lesbian, gay, and bisexual person in our society has internalized an entire complex structure of homophobic and heterosexist attitudes, values, practices, and even institutions. Lesbian/gay/bisexual Christians have internalized an even stronger message of sin and shame which underscore and uphold the internalized homophobic messages from society. It is a wonder that within this environment there can be any psychologically and spiritually healthy gay/lesbian/bisexual people. Yet we are there, helping one another to externalize others' projected messages of shame and sin, differentiating them from the experience of sin and incompleteness that all humans share before God, and celebrating our healthy selves, called to relationships of love and affection, in the name and image of God.

Perhaps the value of family systems and object relations theories for those who wish to end homophobia in the United Church of Christ and other denominations, seeking to move the church at large to a truly Open and Affirming position, can be found in the words of family therapist Paul Watzlovick: "I never saw anyone change by him or her self."[24] In theological terms one might say that faithful individuals need a faithful church in order to change, move, and grow into the will and way of God.

Questions for Discussion

1. What role and positions have gay/lesbian/bisexual persons played in your experience of the church?

2. Can you give an example of a situation in which the concerns of gay/lesbian/bisexual people changed the interactions within a church system?

3. What actions/reactions to gay/lesbian/bisexual concerns have occurred in your congregation? What actions need to take place to create justice? What reactions might you anticipate?

4. What rigid responses to the issue of homosexuality and/or to the coming out of gay/lesbian/bisexual persons do you see in your church? What about within yourself (if you are heterosexual)? What rigid responses have you received (if you are gay/lesbian/bisexual)?

5. Do you experience the church as a functional or dysfunctional system? What are the rules that prevent people from talking about conflicted or emotional issues?

6. How can a faithful church help faithful individuals to grow and change? How can faithful individuals help a faithful church to grow and change? Where do you see yourself in this process?

4···

A Liberating Theology of the Church

The conflict I have experienced throughout my life as a lesbian Christian has never been between my faith in or experience of God, and my acceptance and celebration of my sexual orientation. Even when I first began to utter the word *lesbian* in my mind some twenty years ago, I felt that God was with me, and that naming this identity was somehow a sacred act. Nonetheless, like so many others, I have experienced conflict. This conflict has always been between my acceptance of myself as a lesbian and my experience of the church's nonacceptance in regard to its beliefs and treatment of lesbian/gay/bisexual persons.

Ever since I was a child, the church has been home, especially through the rough years of adolescence and early adulthood. As I struggled with many issues, the church was a healing presence. Through the church I experienced warmth and nurture, mystery and grandeur, community and caring. In the church I learned about the importance of being active in mission, working for justice, and standing up for what I believed. The church taught me that I was made in the image of the Creator, just as I am, a loved and precious child of God. In the church of my childhood I memorized hymns celebrating who I was, this beloved child of God. Sadly, the church has also caused me the greatest pain of rejection, self-denigration, self-denial, confusion, fear, and shame that I have ever known.

I have made two covenants with the church, one at confirmation and the other at ordination. Before this, my parents made a covenant on my behalf at my infant baptism. Because the church is a covenantal community, I take my own vows and the communal covenantal relationship very seriously. As James Nelson writes, "The church is . . . created in and through covenant, the relationship of promise and response between God and the people, and among persons themselves. In genuine community there is always an ongoing conversation among the covenanting parties who are free as unique, distinct, and personal beings to interact with each other."[1]

It is, in part, my faithfulness to the covenants that I have made, combined with Nelson's understanding of the continuity of covenanting parties, that keeps me present and involved in the life of the church.

As someone active in the lesbian/gay/bisexual social and political community, I continually come across persons who ask me why I continue to bother with the church—that is, why "seek approval," why remain in dialogue, why continue in any relationship, let alone seek a call to full-time ministry within and on behalf of an institution that has been so oppressive and abusive to lesbian/gay/bisexual persons for so many generations.

In this chapter I hope to offer some of the images, metaphors, and beliefs that keep me connected to my covenant and to the covenantal community. These are not approval-seeking images, for approval is not what I or most of the lesbian/gay/bisexual Christians with whom I am in conversation want. Rather, these are images of seeking right relationship and making justice as God's children. These images, metaphors, and beliefs are not new or particularly unique. In fact, they are central to the biblical writings and motifs. However, as they are reimaged and rerelated by one who has been marginalized by both church and society, it is hoped that they will offer new hope and understanding to those who ask "Why bother?" These scriptural images are critical to the work of building the liberating community.

In the next chapter I will present a liberation theological model for gay/lesbian/bisexual persons seeking to remain in relation to the institutional church. This liberation theology and spirituality emerges out of the praxis (action and reflection) of working for sexual justice in church and society. Essentially, chapters 4 and 5 are linked by the commitment to justice. However, chapter 4 provides the biblical and theological grounding for the journey toward liberation that takes place in chapter 5.

I have divided this chapter into five sections, each of which addresses a critical aspect of the call of the faithful community in scripture. These are:

1. The church is a community that is both called and led.
2. The church is a worshiping community, whose liturgy is born out of the call of God to struggle against and leave behind an enslaved existence.
3. The church is a community in exile.
4. The church is the community of faith, born out of the experience of deliverance, and called to a covenant of liberation with all of God's creation.
5. The church is the embodiment of Christ

As is noted throughout the text, some of these concepts and images of the faithful community come from the writings of others. However, most have emerged out of my own experience as a pastor and person of faith.

The Church as a Community Both Called and Led

It is important to begin with the understanding of the church as a community that is both called and led. The church has its foundational roots in the historical and theological call to leave behind shackles of injustice, enslavement, suffering, and oppression.

> Then [God] said, "I have observed the misery of my people who are in Egypt; I have heard their cry on account of their taskmasters. Indeed, I know of their sufferings, and I have come down to deliver them from the Egyptians, and to bring them up out of that land into a good and broad land, a land flowing with milk and honey. . . . The cry of the Israelites has now come to me; I have also seen how the Egyptians oppress them. So come, I will send you [Moses] to Pharaoh to bring my people . . . out of Egypt. . . . I will be with you; and this shall be a sign for you that it is I who sent you: when you have brought the people out of Egypt, you shall worship God on this mountain." (Exod. 3:7–12)

The Church as a Worshiping Community

The church is a worshiping community, whose liturgy is born out of the call of God to struggle against and leave behind an enslaved existence. The call to leave oppression is a communal call, as is the call to worship and thank God for our having left oppression behind. Moses does not leave his taskmasters by himself; he is not called in isolation; he is only called within the context of the community. It is the community which is called to liberation, and God empowers Moses within and through the context of his community of faith.

The call is multifaceted, with significant layers of meanings and manifestations. Specifically, it is political. Moses and his people were called to fight against the "powers and principalities" of their day, to take on the gods of the Egyptians, who established the ruling class and structure of slavery.

The call is also economic. By being enslaved, the Israelites performed integral tasks which supported the economics of the society. In the act of leaving bondage, they must have destabilized the economy profoundly.

The call is spiritual. One cannot separate the act of worship from the act of liberation. In fact, in this scripture, the call to worship comes as a result of the journey toward liberation.

This compassionate, frightening, and empowering call of God to leave behind social, political, and spiritual oppression and enslavement is the grounding of the Jewish and Christian traditions and spirituality. Ours is a historical faith rooted in the concrete everyday realities of oppressed and hurting people. We do not come from "wealthy stock"—we come from the poor and marginalized.

This understanding of the foundation of our communal faith has significant implications for the concerns of lesbian/gay/bisexual persons. For example, if we are called to leave behind the taskmasters' oppression in order to gain right worship and relationship with God, then naming the sources of homophobia and heterosexism becomes a critical act of faith. It also becomes an act of faith to leave those taskmasters behind. Leaving behind or walking out of the church because of its homophobic oppression has been something that gay/lesbian/bisexual persons have done for generations. However, walking out in isolation is not the call—the call is communal. One may understand the community as other lesbian/gay/bisexual persons, or one may understand the community as another segment of the larger community of faith in which lesbian/gay/bisexual persons can trust that we are welcome (e.g., the Metropolitan Community Church, an ONA congregation, a gay/lesbian/bisexual church start). The structure and understanding of our faith can feel confusing when we experience both the community and the taskmasters as being one and the same.

This passage also raises questions about the place of heterosexual persons in the journey toward the liberation of gay/lesbian/bisexual persons. Specifically, the call in this passage is for the liberation of the community. I would contend that the taskmasters and the gods of Egypt represent the ideologies of homophobia and heterosexism themselves. Therefore, not only do gay/lesbian/bisexual persons need to be liberated from homophobic oppression within the church, but the community of the church needs to be liberated from heterosexism and homophobia. There are many who have been and will continue to be Moses in this journey. But the journey is not complete with only part of the community, and the liturgy cannot be true worship unless there is liberation. As Gary Comstock writes:

> The church or any community is a dead and nonresurrected body without us. For lesbians and gay men to return to and live within the church without declaring, celebrating, and sharing their affectional identities would make as little sense as reading and remembering the Exodus story and omitting any references to slavery. . . . Without us the church is partial. Together we can get on with the business of building community and making justice and peace.[2]

Another aspect of this passage about the journey toward liberation arises from its political, economic, and spiritual manifestations. By remaining enslaved, the Israelites supported the political, economic, and spiritual status quo. As more and more gay/lesbian/bisexual persons, along with their friends and families, come out of the closet, the challenge to these structures becomes clear.

I, as a clergywoman successfully serving a local parish, came out publicly and loudly because I had sat through one too many discussions about how it was "okay for homosexuals to be in the church, just as it is okay for prostitutes and anyone to be in the church. But it certainly is not okay for them to be pastors or leaders." Although this is not a verbatim quotation, it paraphrases the essence of a speech given by a clergyperson during a debate at the New Hampshire Conference annual meeting in 1989, the year the conference voted to urge local congregations to become "open and affirming of lesbian/gay/bisexual persons."

At that point I became tired of bearing a heavy load for my taskmasters—as have many lesbian/gay/bisexual persons who have been serving the church for generations as teachers, pastors, musicians, moderators, and in all leadership positions. To challenge the heterosexism within the church is to challenge its political, economic, and spiritual structures and assumptions, just as the Hebrews' liberation from slavery challenged the Egyptians. This is a psychological and systemic challenge, as well as a theological one.

As was stated in chapter 3, the structure of interactions and exchanges tends to be complementary and is maintained through enduring patterns. Thus, for example, there exists a complementary relationship and pattern of interaction between church leaders who voice their condemnation of homosexuality, those who are silently complicit in homophobic policies and patterns, and lesbian/gay/bisexual persons who remain closeted in order to remain in the institution. Because of the complementarity inherent in the system, challenging the assumptions of both the "taskmasters" and the "slaves" will throw the entire system into chaos. The biblical story of the Israelites' liberation describes significant chaos throughout the movement toward freedom; this chaos ranges from the sending of the plagues to the parting of the Red Sea. As the church confronts issues related to gay/lesbian/bisexual persons, the chaos may range from the leadership void created when persons refuse to remain closeted in order to serve the church, to conflicted theological disagreements in previously nonconflicted parishes. To challenge the assumptions of the taskmasters is a theological and psychosocial undertaking which will be met with great resistance.

Just as it is critical to understand that the church is the community called out of bondage through the leading of God, it is also significant to understand the purpose and character of this call. Essentially, the people called to liberation are not called to a kind of narcissistic, self-promoting, self-deliverance. Rather, their deliverance is in covenant with all of God's creation.

Sometimes when I question whether I and other gay/lesbian/bisexual advocates are on a self-directed and self-centered road rather than responding to God's call to seek justice, I remember something that happened a few years ago which makes me think again. I had been asked to preach during women's week at a nearby UCC church. As the time drew closer, I began to get anxious, since I had not yet heard back from one of the pastors to make final arrangements. When she did call, she rather self-consciously asked me to promise that I would not mention anything about my sexual orientation from the pulpit. Although I had not planned to make my own sexual orientation the focus of the sermon, I refused to promise anything about what I would or would not say and reminded this pastor about the importance of freedom of the pulpit. When I did not cooperate with her request, she withdrew her invitation to me and offered it to someone else. I imagine that the laywoman she invited seemed like a "safe" choice/replacement. After all, she had been elected "Mother of the Year" at one point and was very active in women's communal programs. Evidently, this new preacher decided that it was important to raise the numbers of ways that women in the church were oppressed, especially lesbian clergy! Needless to say, this upset a few people in the congregation. Honestly, she did not know what had transpired prior to her invitation. However, when I saw her at another church event, she informed me of the invitation and sermon she had preached. So I told her of my prior interactions, and we both laughed aloud, proclaiming and celebrating a divinely inspired and led journey that is bigger and more profound than either of our individual lives might suggest. The work of creating justice for lesbian/gay/bisexual people is a part of our covenantal faith, calling us to create a more just and peaceful world, moved by the vision of God's dominion.

This idea of covenant and covenantal relation is significant throughout all of scripture. However, one image that speaks especially to the call for inclusive rather than particular justice comes from the prophet Isaiah, in some very familiar passages. Every Christmas, churches gather in worship to read Isaiah's visions of justice and peace, which include the images of the lion and lamb lying down together and the little child who shall lead us. One passage in particular describes the inclusive vision of justice:

> On this mountain the [God] of hosts will make for all peoples a feast of rich food, a feast of well-aged wines, of rich food filled with marrow, of well-aged wines strained clear. And [God] will destroy on this mountain the shroud that is cast over all peoples, the sheet that is spread over all nations; [God] will swallow up death forever. Then the [Sovereign] God will wipe away tears from faces, and the disgrace of [God's] people [God] will take away from all the earth. (Isa. 25:6–8)

One cannot escape the numerous references to "all people" made repeatedly throughout this passage. It is clear that God's vision of justice is not particular to any one group; and, therefore, no one is excluded.

There was a poster on the altar during a recent worship service at Spirit of the Mountains that read, "No one is free when others are oppressed." Perhaps this summarizes the vocational call of the church. It is not enough to seek only the liberation of lesbian/gay/bisexual persons, but there can never be enough justice without it.

> The community of faith in the Bible is the people called. It is the people called from diverse sorts of bondage to freedom, called to

a sense of identity founded on a common bond with the God of righteousness and compassion, and called to the twin vocations of worship and participation in the creative, redemptive purpose . . . directed to the restoration of the whole creation.[3]

According to this understanding, it is critical to the essence of the liberation community that diversity be honored. Dividing and separating those who have been oppressed simply continues the experience of alienation. In the social, political, economic, and religious work for justice, the importance of unity and the celebration of diversity are moving into the forefront. Coalitions uniting person of various ethnic backgrounds, economic status, sexual orientations, and other differences that have traditionally divided humanity are beginning to come together to work for political and social justice.

Audre Lorde, an African American lesbian feminist, describes in *Sister Outsider* the flavor of this movement, explaining that we reveal ourselves "in work and struggle together with those whom we define as different from ourselves," to create "patterns for relating across our human differences as equals; [we] do not have to become like each other in order to work together for a future [we] will all share."[4]

One might think that the church could lead such an inclusive movement for justice. Sadly, however, it is exactly the church that seems to fall behind in this inclusivity. Perhaps more sobering is the reality that this is not the first generation to note the church's falling behind in the work for justice and inclusivity.

> The church has lost the chance to become the unifying element in our American society. It is not anticipating new facts. It is merely catching up slowly to the new social facts created by economic and other forces. . . . What we accomplish in the way of church unity ought to be accepted with humility and not hailed with pride. We are not creating. We are simply catching up with creation.[5]

One might ask why it is so difficult for the church to live out the call to work for the liberation of all creation, since it has been a part of our foundational understanding throughout history. Perhaps it is because seeking seriously to deliver real people from real oppression places one in the midst of real conflict. As this call to inclusive, embracing deliverance from bondage places one in conflict with the "powers and principalities" of our time, it can present a conflict of interest to the institution of the church. Specifically, the sexism, heterosexism, and homophobia which enslave us also uphold much of the political and economic power that the institution and its leaders experience. Thus, this cannot be a conflict that the church, as a system, can easily or clearly undertake. Even though systems are always in a state of dynamic transformation and are never totally static, the system continues to seek homeostasis and stability. Therefore, to be in conflict with itself as well as with the larger suprasystem of political and economic power is a complex and multifaceted endeavor, which requires the broadest possible coalition of support. As a friend once said to me, "I am coming to believe that the church is called to a journey of 'downward mobility,' but how do we do it?"

Theologically, to place oneself and one's community in the struggle for liberation and into conflict with the structure and status quo of power is to place oneself into exile with the Christ. If one is not the community in power, then one becomes the community in exile, as did the Israelites, as did Christ Jesus. Hebrews offers a powerful and painful image of the Christ in exile:

> We have an altar from which those who officiate in the tent have no right to eat. For the bodies of those animals whose blood is brought into the sanctuary by the high priest as a sacrifice for sin are burned outside the camp. Therefore, Jesus also suffered outside the city gate in order to sanctify the people by his own blood. Let us then go to him outside the camp and bear the abuse he endured. (Heb. 13:10–14)

This passage vividly paints the reality of what happens to one who challenges the powers and principalities. Essentially, Jesus is treated as a sacrificial animal, left outside the wall of the city, out of view, away from concern, to die in his own blood. In the beginning of the AIDS crisis—and, sadly, continuing today—

this image is all too descriptive of those who live and die with AIDS. The church systematically has excluded openly gay men from the inside for so long that those with AIDS have usually been left on the outside to die from a disease that attacks their own blood. The truth of Christ Jesus left to die in his own blood outside of the walled city is unfortunately still very real.

This passage not only points to the reality of gay men and others living and dying with AIDS, it is also a powerful symbol of the risk involved in taking seriously the call to work for justice. Who wants to end up on the outside?

The Church as a Community in Exile

In *Today's Church: A Community of Exiles and Pilgrims,* George Webber asserts that the faithful community should be on the outside, in exile: "Exile has become normative for God's people. . . . [I]n exile, they could sing the praises of their God in a strange land. . . . For Christians in an affluent world, in a nation as powerful and self-righteous as the United States, the only rational posture for us must also be one of aliens or exiles."[6] Exile is not about a place. Exile is about a relationship, or lack of relationship. To be in exile is to be removed from the traditional structures, roles, and positions of power.

To illustrate this point, I remember a time when I was a parish pastor in a socially and politically conservative area. The church I was serving had voted itself a Peace with Justice Congregation and was beginning to engage in an Open and Affirming (ONA) study process. The church had a reputation in the community for being "liberal" and active in social ministry. One of the most outspoken supporters of this direction for the church was someone who appears to fit the more traditional stereotype (i.e., a white, straight, fifty-year-old, wealthy male). At one point, he came to me expressing feelings of confusion and loneliness. He related that his friends with whom he had grown up and his business colleagues of the past twenty years were telling him that they thought he was "crazy." He said they did not understand his politics, his religion, or anything he be-

lieved anymore. They did not really want to be around him anymore, because he was not like them anymore. This caring and
faithful man was expressing great pain as he began to experience social, political, and economic isolation. Yet he assured me
that he felt more spiritual and faithful than he ever had.

The place of exile inevitably brings one into conflict with
the assumptions of the present power structure. It is a place
from which one can rarely, if ever, turn back. It is the place of
sacred faith, within the tradition of the historical call of God to
set the captives free: "For freedom, Christ has set us free; stand
fast therefore, and do not submit again to a yoke of slavery"
(Gal. 5:1).

It is one experience of faith to be a part of a religious community that understands itself as one body in exile together. It
is quite another experience to live an exiled existence within
the community of faith itself. For the lesbian/gay/bisexual person of Christian faith, the experiences of invisibility, marginalization, and condemnation are normative, not only in spite of
the church, but often in the name of, because of, and within the
church.

Gay/lesbian/bisexual persons are not, however, the only
ones to know the experience of being made invisible by those
already on the margin. People of color, disabled persons, low-
income women and children, and others also know this reality.
Although the story of each individual and each particular group
is unique, the experience of oppression by the community
called to liberation is much the same.

The most painful and confusing aspect of this experience of
oppression within the context of the faith community arises
from the language and imagery often employed by religious
leaders. More than any other institution, the church is constantly
using the words *love, family, acceptance, grace, salvation,* and
hope. One of the church's functions is to celebrate rituals and
sacraments of covenanting and uniting all of God's children.
And yet, in these very rituals, sacraments, and metaphors les-
bian/gay/bisexual persons are excluded repeatedly, both by in-
tention and lack of attention.

The Church as the Community of Faith, Called to a Covenant of Liberation with All Creation

The church is the community of faith, born out of the experience of deliverance, and called to a covenant of liberation with all of God's creation. At this point in history, the church must look internally at itself, at the ways in which it exiles its own faithful, if its worship is ever to be a sign of the healing and hope of God.

Comstock explains, "Both the Exodus and the life, death, and resurrection of Jesus are events or stories about overcoming and transforming pain, suffering, and death. Christians as people who are born of these events, therefore, are not those who bear or endure pain; they are those who transform it."[7] If the community of faith is called to deliver all people out of oppression, enslavement, and pain, then who can we understand ourselves to be as we journey through the wilderness toward the promised land?

The Church as the Embodiment of the Christ

Now there are varieties of gifts, but the same Spirit; and there are varieties of services, but the same [God]. . . . To each is given the manifestation of the Spirit for the common good. . . . All these are activated by one and the same Spirit. . . . For just as the body is one and has many members, and all of the members of the body, though many, are one body—Jews or Greek, slaves or free—and we were all made to drink of one Spirit. Indeed, the body does not consist of one member, but of many. If the foot were to say, "Because I am not a hand, I do not belong to the body," that would not make it any less a part of the body. . . . If the whole body were an eye, where would the hearing be? . . . The eye cannot say to the hand, "I have no need of you." . . . If one member suffers, all suffer together with it; if one member is honored, all rejoice together with it. Now you are the body of Christ and individually members of it. (1 Cor. 12:4–27, selected verses)

This scriptural message is compelling in its image of what it is to be a community of faith. It is the *body* of Christ that is called to liberation, to worship, and to community. We are called to an enacted, embodied journey of faith together. This is not an otherwordly, anti-body, ethereal picture of religiosity.

In *Embodiment,* James Nelson discusses the importance of the metaphor of the body of Christ in dealing with sexual ethics:

> The [b]ody of Christ is thus antithetical to any spiritual dualism. It is not a community of discarnate spirits, but of body-selves bound to each other in and through their incarnate Lord. The church as body is also antithetical to sexist dualism. . . . Those deeply involved in the women's movement testify that sisterhood means a redemptive and revelatory cohumanity. It is a therapeutic community, enabling women to deal with their repressed alienation. It is a supportive community which counters isolation, a healing community which allows its members to find their strength in solidarity with each other. But sisterhood is also an image which transcends biological gender. It points to the body which the church as a whole is called to be.[8]

In order to be and become the body of Christ together, we must acknowledge the significance of our body-selves. We must establish a practice of faith in which all who seek it may find a safe place to deal with our human histories of alienation, to find strength with others, to give meaning to our common and unique realities of being human, and to know that indeed we are "each given the manifestation of the Spirit for the common good" (1 Cor. 12:7).

In order to do this, we must not be afraid to deal with the realities of living within bodies. I cannot count how many times I have heard people say that the church is simply not relevant to the issues that concern people's time, energy, thoughts, and emotional lives. I believe that people most often feel this way about the areas of sex and sexuality. Having been a part of two congregations as they began to talk about the ONA study process, one difficulty became clear over and over again. That is, people felt as though they were being asked to make a decision about something that they had never before talked about (and perhaps not even thought about) in church. Essentially, people were brought into the midst of a controversial discussion and potential vote about homosexuality, without ever having thought about or engaged with others in studying a theology of sexuality or embodiment. I remember in one parish where I served, the joke at the deacons' meeting was that after people began to mention the words *Open and Affirming,* people went scurrying off to their Bibles as never before. I believe that these people were looking frantically for some guidance in an area about which the church has been silent at best and oppressive at worst.

> The call to the church in this era is to be present with its people. . . [and] to assist in the search for behavior patterns that will enhance the lives of all people The time has come for the church, if it wishes to have any credibility as a relevant institution, to look at the issues of single people, divorcing people, post-married people, and gay and lesbian people from a point of view removed from the patriarchal patterns of the past, and to help these people find a path that leads to a life-affirming holiness.[9]

Ours is an incarnational faith. A part of the foundation of the Christian religion is that God chose to become human in the historical person of Jesus. As we say together in the UCC statement of faith, "In Jesus Christ, the man of Nazareth, our crucified and risen savior, you have come to us and shared our common lot." Therefore, it seems clear that if the church is truly to be the embodiment of the Christ in this day and age, then we must move toward all people, sharing their common lot. In other words, we must be about the work of incarnating a faith that is real and relevant. In particular, we must begin more appropriately to engage simultaneously in two equally significant ministries. First, we must incarnate the spirit of the Christ into the life of the community as diverse, inclusive, justice-seeking love. Second, we must reach out to the real needs of real people who seek to live lives of healing and wholeness within the context of their body-selves. We must take one another seriously and invite all of God's children to participate and contribute, so that we may celebrate the fullness of creation.

In summary, it is clear from scripture that we are called to function as the body of Christ, diverse and inclusive, as we journey together, seeking the liberation of all of God's creation, so that our worship and relationships may be right and true. As I stated in the beginning of this chapter, none of this is particularly new; most of it comes from scripture. However, just as the choice was to become relevant and real in the incarnation of Christ Jesus, we have an ongoing choice for relevancy and realness in the day-to-day living out of our call to be the church. Unfortunately, the church seems to move slowly in making these changes and choices, as Webber explains:

> There are few institutions in our society whose form and patterns of operation have been as slow to change as those in the church. There is a strong predisposition to believe that ecclesiastical structures as we know them are God-given and eternal. Thus, they are not subject to any serious change. Yet, the whole history of the church reflects a very different pattern. In each new historical era the attempt to be faithful to the gospel has driven the churches to adopt new ecclesiastical forms and new patterns of life.[10]

It is my prayer, and the prayer of many others with whom I have spoken, worked, cried, laughed, sung, marched, loved, and prayed that the church will someday change the old forms and patterns that have for so long hurt lesbian/gay/bisexual persons and have hurt the church as a whole. To function as the body of Christ, we must move beyond the institutional structures which support the god of heterosexist ideology. We must leave Egypt, together, walking our God-given journey toward liberation. Then and only then will we be able to say, "Now you are the body of Christ, and individually members of it" (1 Cor. 12:27).

Questions for Discussion

1. If you are gay, lesbian, or bisexual, in what ways have you experienced the church as liberative, oppressive, or both? If you are heterosexual, how has the church, in your experience, been liberative and oppressive to gay, lesbian, and bisexual people?

2. How have the roles of taskmasters and slaves been played out?

3. What does your own congregation state is its call as a community of faith?

4. How do worship and liturgy reflect (or not) the concerns of justice, liberation, inclusivity, and diversity?

5. Often gay/lesbian/bisexual people have stated that support groups, music groups, and recovery groups function more like "church" than the institutional church ever has. Given this, what community do you find the closest to "church" as described in this chapter? Is it different from the church of your childhood? If so, how?

6. Who lives in exile within and around your church? How are you in exile?

7. What might be the marks of a faithful covenantal church in your area?

5···

The Journey toward Sexual
and Spiritual Liberation

The Christian church in general and the United Church of Christ in particular are intergenerational, long-established, systems with enduring boundaries, patterns of operation, interaction, and beliefs. This long history affects the vitality and relevancy of their theology. Although the term *theology* may have different meanings to different people, it is traditionally understood as the study of the nature of God. Theology is the way in which we speak and think about God and God's relationship to humanity and all of creation. For too long, both theology and the position from which one engages in it have been handed down from one generation to the next without the emerging generation appropriating and claiming theology for itself. In addition, the work of theology and theologizing has often been removed from the day-to-day living of many who make up the church.

As a clergyperson in various settings, I have known many laypeople to turn to me as the "expert" rather than trust their own opinions and beliefs. I have also known too many clergy who are quite comfortable in the role of the expert, unwilling to be challenged by others. Specifically, persons in positions of power in the church have studied and written theology and handed it over to the rest of humanity. As we saw in chapters 1 and 3, these positions of power are based on and held in place by sexist and heterosexist belief systems. Therefore, women, lesbian/gay/bisexual persons and others who do not fit the traditional "white, straight, male" criteria for positions of power have been and continue to be excluded from the doing of theology, as it relates to systemic understandings and actualizations of faith.

In *A Theology of Liberation,* Gustavo Gutiérrez describes two functions of classical theology: theology as wisdom and theology as rational knowledge:

> Theology as wisdom . . . was essentially a meditation on the Bible. . . . Distinctions were made between the "beginners," the faithful, and the "advanced," who sought perfection. . . . This theology was above all monastic and therefore . . . removed from worldly concerns. . . . From the twelfth century on, theology began to establish itself as a science . . . to define, present, and explain revealed truths, to examine doctrines . . . to teach revealed truths authoritatively.[1]

Gutiérrez contrasts this with what he calls "theology as critical reflection on praxis." This kind of theology arises from concern with a particular set of issues that emerges as critical reflection on action within the lives and experiences of faithful people. In this light, the political hermeneutic of the gospel calls us to be "engaged where nations, social classes, people struggle to free themselves from domination and oppression"[2].

Liberation theology and spirituality, as a school of theological work and experience (rather than as a school of thought), have emerged as a powerful voice within and outside of the institution of the church. Perhaps the most articulate original voices of liberation theology emerged out of the struggle for economic justice, peace, and liberation in the poor countries of Latin America during the 1960s and 1970s. This kind of political theology of praxis arose primarily from the barrios of South and Central America, where people were trying to reconcile the poverty, violence, and warfare of their lives with the classical teachings of their faith and to appropriate the gospel for their times.

My own firsthand experience of this kind of faith and theology occurred in March 1983. Having just completed my seminary studies, I decided to travel to Nicaragua with Witness for Peace (an ecumenical nonviolent organization focused on sending U.S. citizens to witness firsthand the effects of U.S. policy in Nicaragua). The purpose of this trip was to observe the effects of the United States–sponsored *Contra* War on the people of

Nicaragua and to stand as a nonviolent presence in the midst of the conflict. In fairly typical "Norte Americana" style, I was fresh out of theological school and thought I knew most everything about theology—even liberation theology, since I has taken a course in it. I was totally unprepared for the power, articulateness, and integrity of faith of the people I met.

While there, we spent some time in Jalapa, a small town bordering Honduras. Virtually every family in this town had lost someone to the guerilla warfare waged by the *Contras*. I went to worship in one of the *"comunidades de base"* (Christian base communities), whose leadership included the organizers of the Mothers of Martyrs and Heroes and a renegade priest. In this service of worship, no one was preached to. Instead, the people listened to the scripture and responded by expressing what they believed it meant for them and their struggle. People spoke of the harsh realities of their lives—running nightly into bomb shelters, losing children to machine-gun fire in their own homes, being unable to farm because of *Contra* attacks. They also spoke of the realities of the organized church, referring to the collusion of wealthy church leaders with the economic forces of the *Contras*. These people were committed to justice and peace, and their theology emerged from the realities of their communal lives. The antipolitical, otherworldy theology they had been taught in the traditional structure and organization of the church had not made sense in their situation. Their lives were already politicized and very earthly. The question was whether their theology would be relevant. As Gutiérrez says:

> It is for all these reasons that the theology of liberation offers us not so much a new theme for reflection as a new way to do theology. Theology as critical reflection on historical praxis is a liberating theology. . . . This is a theology that does not stop with reflecting on the world, but rather tries to be a part of the process through which the world is transformed. It is a theology that is open—in the protest against trampled human dignity, in the struggle against the plunder of the vast majority of people, in liberating love, and in the building of a new, just, and [brotherly/sisterly] society—to the gift of the kingdom of God.[3]

Latin America is not the only place that liberation theology has been happening. Across the world, people are creating their own *comunidades de base* that speak out of the particularities of their existence. Theology from the "underside" has been happening for generations. However, until recently, the exchange of information about theology from one position to another has been mostly one-sided, that is *from* classical texts and positions of power *to* the majority of the faithful.

One place in which theology from the underside is emerging to speak faithfully out of its life experience is in the gay/lesbian/bisexual community. Lesbian/gay/bisexual liberation theology is developing as a powerful and profound school of theological work and thought. It is one among many communities from which new voices of faith are speaking out about the vast chasm between the praxis of our lives and the teachings of classical theology. My intent in this chapter is to raise a voice of hope and liberation in the journey toward the full reign of God.

My own journey toward a spirituality of liberation began similarly to that of many gay/lesbian/bisexual persons raised in Christianity. As a young child active in church school, I was taught repeatedly that if I gave my heart to Jesus, I would know the freedom of new life in Christ. As an adult, I have come to disagree radically with many of the overspiritualized tenets and patriarchal world view of the teachings I experienced. Yet, I still believe there is powerful, life-giving truth in this statement. Its power is profound because when misused, it can become a litmus test for who is "in" and who is "out" of the dominion of God, and can give rise to oppressive, violent systems of control and alienation. (Men are "in," women are "out," heterosexuals are "in," gay/lesbian/bisexual/transgendered people are "out," white people are "in," people of color are "out," Americans are "in," those from elsewhere are "out.")

This spiritual power can be oppressive, yet it can also be healing. It is life-giving when the community seeks together to embody the passion of the inclusive and liberating love of the Christ in the here and now of this world. It is life-giving and liberating to share my heart's passion for justice and love with

Jesus, the one who lived as my brother, taking on the powers and principalities of his day and empowering the poor and marginalized. It is life-giving, liberating, and healing to join my heart and hands with the hearts and hands of others as we work, cry, pray, sing, make love, march, laugh, meet, and organize for justice. When we break bread together in worship, in potluck suppers, in hospital rooms, and on the street corner in a parade, the risen Christ is in our midst, and we know new life.

If there is to be any integrity, any truth, any reality to the assertion of "new life in Christ Jesus" for lesbian/gay/bisexual persons, then we must be about creating and living a theology and spirituality of liberation in our midst. To engage in the task of gay/lesbian/bisexual liberation theology is to acknowledge that the old voices that taught many of us no longer resonate. It is to state that the metaphors, images, and belief systems of white, heterosexual, academic men in positions of power within the church and society often lack connection to the theological, political, social, relational, and economic realities of lesbian/gay/bisexual persons within this society. As stated I earlier, gay/lesbian/bisexual persons need to speak, to tell our stories in order to be faithful. Likewise, those who have been speaking about theology for generations need to listen for the voice of God in the voices of others.

Gay/lesbian/bisexual persons need to acknowledge the particularity of our existence and of everyone else's, for each of us must each speak out of his/her own experience, in his/her own voice, and hopefully raise our voices together in a harmonious choir. As Carter Heyward proclaimed, "The words I speak—whether about grocery shopping, Anglican spirituality, sex, or Christ—are lesbian-feminist words because I speak them."[4] I believe that the work of gay/lesbian/bisexual spirituality of liberation is to claim and create worship, prayer, social and political action, a life focus, and spiritual discipline that celebrate who we are as sexual-spiritual children of God.

This theology/spirituality of liberation is not to be confused with a systematic "liberal" theology, with its emphasis on rational discourse and disengagement. Rather, it is to be a reflection of the spiritual empowerment in the real lives of lesbian/gay/bisexual persons, seeking to survive and thrive within the confines of a heterosexist and homophobic church and society.

Coming out theologically is an act of radical faith, seeking spiritual connectedness to our concrete, day-to-day realities. Coming out theologically is just as much an act of deviance and resistance as is coming out socially and politically. When we speak our truth as we experience it, communally and individually, we move out of isolation and celebrate what is particular as well as what is universal. When we speak, not only do we move out of isolation and alienation from not only the "powers and principalities" of this world, but we lay claim and voice to the spiritual empowerment that is both immanent and transcendent. Finally, to engage in a theology of liberation for lesbian/gay/bisexual persons is to take theology seriously, rather than to dismiss it as meaningless and hopeless, thereby resigning ourselves to theological and spiritual apathy.

I know that in my own journey as a lesbian feminist Christian the most profoundly spiritual moments in my life have been those times when I have been intimately connected with others and when together we have spoken our truth loudly and boldly, celebrating and proclaiming who we are, and calling for the creation of justice in church and society. Did others hear us? I am not sure. Nor am I sure that it mattered. What mattered was that we spoke, and in the act of speaking, history was changed. As we shall see in the interviews in chapter 6, this reality is true for many with whom I have spoken. That is, the most profound spiritual moments for many lesbian/gay/bisexual persons have been in connection with others seeking and speaking up for sexual justice.

This healing power proclaimed by lesbian/gay/bisexual persons coming together in community to speak the reality of our lives points to the intimate connection between a theology of liberation and a psychology that is liberating. Two points about the psychological realities of lesbian/gay/bisexual persons have been raised repeatedly throughout this book.

The first point concerns the role and position that lesbian/gay/bisexual persons have played systemically in both the church and society. For generations, lesbian/gay/bisexual persons have been placed in the role of the shame-bearers, carrying sexualized guilt, shame, evil, and sin for the system. When people speak of us as "sick," "perverted," "sinful," "abominations," etc., they are, in the understanding of systems theory, projecting clear and direct feedback to lesbian/gay/bisexual persons about our place in the system. This projection, or pattern of interaction, has endured over time and is built into the very core of the beliefs, values, and norms that uphold the tenacity of the system itself.

The second point concerns the assertion of systems theory that our interactions with our contexts shape and influence our identities as unique individuals. In other words, I learn who I am by what my environment tells me. Therefore, the homophobic and heterosexist messages interwoven into the system of the church and society tell the lesbian/gay/bisexual person that she/he is not whole, holy, or worthy. Therefore, lesbian/gay/bisexual persons cannot help but internalize some of this message of shame and guilt, theologically and psychologically. The power of projective identification is very strong within a system such as the church. This internalization leads, psychologically, to a fragmented sense of self, which often can be healed only within the context of a new system. Theologically, this leads to a sense of knowing oneself as the "inferior part of the body of Christ," unworthy and unable to know God's love without denying who one really is.

Several years ago while I was serving as a local church pastor, a gay man told me that he felt completely unable to walk inside a church sanctuary after having come out. This was true despite the fact (and perhaps because of it) that he had been a very active deacon and choir member while he was married to a woman. He knew that several gay and lesbian persons were active in the congregation, and in his mind he kept telling himself that he should feel okay about his sexuality and his religion. Nonetheless, every time he stepped inside a church, he began to feel physically ill and thought of himself as a condemned and horrible person.

I believe that this points to how deeply and unconsciously the messages of shame and guilt are embedded, psychologically and theologically. In isolation, our rational minds cannot extricate them. Neither can we externalize these projections if we are in an organization in which others do not feel a responsibility to withdraw their own homophobic and heterosexist projections. Again, if gay/lesbian/bisexual church members are expected to participate in the congregation with a healthy sense of faith and identity, then heterosexual members must do their own work on homophobia and heterosexism. To do otherwise simply creates another version of injustice. Lesbian/gay/bisexual persons need a new community or system of voices that externalizes the shame and message of sin in order to create a whole sense of self in relation to the body of Christ. The church can choose to be a part of this healing journey or to continue its collusion in oppressing lives and souls.

As one member of Spirit of the Mountains stated, "I used to be a member of a homophobic church. I tried to be like they wanted—nice, polite, compromising, not demanding too much. I tried being comfortable being invisible, even though they were the ones who initially made an issue out of my lesbianism. I tried to be patient when they said that raising the topic of Open and Affirming would split the church. I finally chose to get out. I have better things to do with my life than comfort them in their hypocrisy and homophobia."

At present, there is a profound movement toward liberation within the lesbian/gay/bisexual community, which is being manifested politically, socially, psychologically, and theologically. One of the clearest symbols of the strength of this movement is the March on Washington that took place in April 1993. Organizers say that there were almost one million people marching that day, although media estimates were lower (as they have been with every national gay/lesbian/bisexual march). As a participant, I found myself overwhelmed, surprised, awed, and inspired all day long. Prior to this, I could only imagine that there were this many of us out there—each working for justice in his/her own time and place. Now I know that within every trade, profession, state, and ethnic group, we are there, along with others, speaking up and working toward a vision of justice. The March on Washington was a show of strength, as in the words of Holly Near's song "We Are a Gentle, Angry People."

Because liberation is a multifaceted movement, there has also begun a ground swell of work for sexual justice within the church. Virtually every denomination from the Catholics to the Mormons was represented by a community of people seeking justice at the March on Washington. When I first came out in the late 1970s, I thought I was completely alone as a lesbian in the church (even though I now know that I was not).

My experience of the United Church Coalition for Lesbian/Gay Concerns (UCCL/GC) is that it has functioned over the years as a kind of community of liberation. Through its work of advocacy on a denominational and interdenominational level, its pastoral support of lesbian/gay/bisexual persons, and its efforts to bring people out of isolation into community, to speak the realities of our existence, and to engage in social and political action, the UCCL/GC has become its own kind of national *comunidad de base,* seeking the liberation of its people.

From this organization, two other movements have taken root and are beginning to flourish (see chapter 2). One of these is the Open and Affirming movement, which became official in 1985, when the UCC General Synod voted to call on local congregations to adopt policies of nondiscrimination with regard to sexual orientation, and encouraged congregations to adopt a "Covenant of Openness and Affirmation [later referred to as O&A] of persons of lesbian, gay, and bisexual orientation within the community of faith." Since then the movement has grown, so that at the time of this writing there are 172 ONA (the preferred acronym) churches, and ten conferences that have passed ONA resolutions. (The movement is growing so rapidly that before this book is published, the numbers will have changed.)

Since 1985 there have also emerged several new church starts, congregations, or worshiping communities with a particular outreach to the lesbian/gay/bisexual community. These congregations do not seek to exclude heterosexuals but rather to create an environment in which those who have been disenfranchised by the church can come together in a new kind of community. They seek to be communities in which all persons, regardless of sexual orientation, are welcome, and in which the specific concerns of living in a heterosexist society are raised in worship and education. At this point, there are four to five such congregations affiliated in some way with the United Church of Christ, including the Spirit of the Lakes in Minneapolis and the City of Hope Church in San Francisco.

Spirit of the Mountains, a gay/straight justice-seeking worshiping community, in Concord, New Hampshire, is one of these communities. Spirit of the Mountains began in December 1991 with a Christmas worship service and potluck supper. Since then, from twenty to sixty people have continued to gather twice a month for worship, supper, and discussions. Sometimes worship follows the liturgical order of the UCC Book of Worship. At other times, participants divide into small groups to reflect on the theme raised in worship. At still other times, we engage in a more "Quaker" style of liturgy, inviting all to join in a time of silence and speak as the Spirit moves.

Although there has been clearly identified pastoral leadership since the beginning, Spirit of the Mountains has sought to maintain itself as a grassroots organization, celebrating the diversity of gifts of all participants. To this end, we have sought training in the process of consensus decision making, written and adopted a corporate mission statement (see appendix A), written and adopted a communal statement declaring ourselves an Open and Affirming, Just Peace Community (see appendix A), and established a working worship committee that meets regularly to offer the pastor input in planning and leading worship. We meet quarterly to discuss our ongoing sense of mission and purpose and to make plans to carry this out. We also publish a regular newsletter to keep persons informed about our actions and decisions as well as to provide information about the gay/lesbian/bisexual community.

In addition, we have sought to be present and active in witnessing for justice in church and society. We have marched as a group in the March on Washington and in the New Hampshire gay/lesbian/bisexual pride celebrations. We have publicly supported the campaign to end discrimination in New Hampshire and have participated in a letter-writing campaign concerning Martin Luther King Jr. Day. In our worship, we provide a time for people to announce rallies or otherwise raise social concerns. We have sold T-shirts to fund the area's "Take Back the Night" march. We have also continued to contribute one-half to one-third of our regular offering to the UCC's Our Church's Wider Mission (OCWM) fund. In addition, we sometimes take extra offerings to support actions of mission and social justice.

Even with all of this, most people involved with Spirit of the Mountains have confirmed that the most significant ministry we have is that of being present and visible within a rural, conservative state. During a recent planning meeting, one member jokingly suggested selling bumper stickers proclaiming, "Spirit of the Mountains: The Biggest Gay Church in New Hampshire." Out of this experience of being present, visible, and active within a conservative, rural state our theology of liberation has been planted, is taking root, and is growing.

In *Lift Every Voice: Constructing Christian Theologies from the Underside,* Susan Brooks Thistlethwaite and Mary Potter Engel describe liberation theologies as communal, prophetic and constructive. "They are also concrete, practical, and historical theologies. . . . Active commitment to a specific struggle for liberation. . . is the first necessary element in this theology. . . . [Liberation theology] is both a theology of protest against unjust social orders and a theology aimed at social transformation toward greater justice for all. . . . [A]nother of the goals . . . is the empowerment of individuals."[5]

One of the difficulties I have experienced in my work for the liberation of lesbian/gay/bisexual persons in the church, as well as for the articulation of a gay/lesbian/bisexual liberation theology, comes from people's appeal to their supposed rationality. Whether making a presentation to a church engaged in the

ONA study process, hearing from parishioners when I was pastoring an almost exclusively heterosexual church, or encouraging lesbian/gay/bisexual persons and their friends and families
to speak up about being silenced and marginalized in the
church, I have often encountered a hesitancy couched in the familiar phrase, "We need to hear from the other side." According
to Thistlethwaite and Engel, the experience of community that
allows for this type of dialogue to have real meaning, rarely if
ever, occurs. Rather, the group that insists on this type of conversation is, more often that not, antithetical to the meaning and
purpose of community. True dialogue can only happen among
equals when the power base is shared.

> While they admit that religious experience is ambiguous and plu-
> ralistic, liberation theologians do not agree that the way forward
> lies through "genuine conversation" or genuine communities of
> inquiry, especially if community is understood as an academic
> guild rather than as the smaller hermeneutical communities of
> shared commitment that are engaged in struggles for justice. . . .
> Community is possible when it begins with the fundamental eq-
> uity of those who are displaced. Without the understanding of
> community, conversation itself becomes but another form of im-
> perialism, with Western, white, privileged persons setting the
> agenda. And when this is the case, liberation theologians are
> choosing not to enter the conversation . . . in order to respond to
> the prior and more urgent needs of justice.[6]

I believe that this understanding of liberation theology presents a key issue in the development of communities such as
Spirit of the Mountains. Far from ghettoizing our experience,
when we come together in a community focused on the concerns of lesbian/gay/bisexual persons, we are providing the opportunity to share our experience as individuals and to be
greeted with respect and affection. It offers us the chance to
move out of isolation, reclaim our true selves, and move into
mutual relation with others to work actively for social transformation. True community is also the time and place through
which we collectively begin to voice our understandings and
beliefs about what it is to journey together as diverse sexual/

spiritual beings made in the image of God. There are several settings beyond the predominantly gay/lesbian/bisexual congregations in which this kind of experience can occur. For example, local churches can provide gay/lesbian/bisexual support and/or study groups.

At Spirit of the Mountains, we prioritize our connection with the larger church and seek actively to maintain that connection through our offering of money, attendance at association and conference events, and through ongoing dialogue with conference leadership as to the meaning and role of Spirit of the Mountains within the larger church. Nevertheless, in a conference with only four ONA churches, spread across the state, we remain firmly committed to providing a safe place for persons to explore and celebrate what it means to be gay/lesbian/bisexual and Christian. In the words of one of the active lay leaders of Spirit of the Mountains, "If the mainstream church could put us out of business by making Spirit of the Mountains unnecessary, we'd be happy to close. Until then, we need to take care of ourselves."

In *Speaking of Christ: A Lesbian-Feminist Voice,* Carter Heyward includes a chapter titled "Living for the Living: Theological Lessons from Nicaragua." In this chapter, she includes four "lessons" from the experiences of the base communities in Nicaragua that are similar to the work for liberation of lesbian/gay/bisexual persons in the United States. The first of these lessons is that "'The living' includes all past, as well as current, inhabitants of planet earth who have been committed to [the] well-being of humanity."[7]

As much as we are working for embodiment of the faith and the denial of spiritual/sexual dualism, the body is not the defining factor in death and life or in someone's participation in liberation. By spiritual/sexual dualism, I mean the unnatural split between someone's physical and spiritual essence. In my journeys to Nicaragua, I have participated in funeral services for victims of the war between the United States–backed *Contras* and the *Sandinistas.* As the names of those who died at the hands of the *Contras* were called out, the congregation shouted,

"*Presente!*"—meaning that even though their bodies were dead, they continued to be present in the work of the community of freedom.

At Spirit of the Mountains, we have sometimes placed on our altar pictures of gay men who have died due to complications from the AIDS virus. Also, when we participate in the sacrament of communion and often during the time of sharing joys and concerns, we remember those who are not with us in body. Sometimes they are remembered by name and at other times by the concern or issue that keeps them away (e.g., those who are too frightened to come to this gathering, those who are overwhelmed by internalized homophobia). One does not always have to be physically present in order to be spiritually and socially connected to those seeking justice.

Heyward observes, "Our problem, our spiritual, social, political, and pastoral problem, is not that we take human life too seriously but that we do not take divine life seriously enough. Thus, we fail to discern the presence of the spirit of love, the source of justice, here in our midst—ours to actualize."[8] This is the other side of the insight that death is not all that it appears, and that those who have died from homophobic violence, AIDS, suicide, and the slow emotional death of internalized homophobia continue to be with us in our struggle for justice.

Life is also more than it appears. A significant step toward liberation for gay/lesbian/bisexual persons is to name and celebrate the divine spirit, energy, presence, and power in our midst. Indeed, to proclaim, as does Carter Heyward, that the "erotic is sacred." For far too long we have been labeled as "sick," "perverted," "evil," "sinful," and "an abomination of God's law." These terms have been used to justify oppression, marginalization, and violence. Therefore, it becomes a spiritual act of resurrection to rise out of these labels and all that they symbolize and live together as the new community of the risen Christ, proclaiming "*Presente!*" in our actions and interactions of love and justice.

Heyward's second lesson is that "The body is, first and foremost, human flesh and blood and bones and mouths and tears which require immediate attention."9 This lesson stands in direct contrast to the classical, academic teaching of theology previously described, which affirms the body as a spiritualized phenomenon. As we observed in chapter 4, the "body of Christ" found in scripture is completely antithetical to spiritual dualism and, therefore, calls us to an embodied, enacted, actualized journey of faith. In order to function as the body of Christ we must acknowledge and act through our body-selves. Liberation is flesh and blood, as we are flesh and blood.

Lesbian/gay/bisexual Christians, even more than heterosexuals, have been taught that the urges, desires, feelings, and pleasures of the body are somehow to be endured, abstained from, or even condemned as inherently bad. Too often we have heard such phrases as, "I can accept you, but not your sexual orientation," or "It's okay to be gay/lesbian, as long as you don't act on it." This is like hearing that it is acceptable to be yourself as long as you don't actualize yourself with any kind of physicality (yet another version of the "Don't act, don't tell" policy).

Therefore, another act of radical liberation for lesbian/gay/bisexual persons is to reclaim the body as good, healing, and holy. It is through our bodies that we live our lives. It was through the body of the man, Jesus, that God became flesh to live among us. It is through the body that the Spirit of God is made incarnate, over and over again.

In the third lesson, Heyward declares: "Our responsibility is to live as interdependent members of a Body—which is to be human, fully human."10 The point of this lesson has been stated previously: that is, that no one struggle for liberation is separate from any other struggle and that "no one is free, while others are oppressed." "For Nicaragua's revolutionary Christians, the Body of Christ is actively whatever Body—person or group—is struggling against unjust suffering. No one person or group of people, be it nation, religious tradition, race, or gender, has a monopoly on being the Body of Christ."11

At Spirit of the Mountains we seek continually to make connections between issues of oppression as well as movements for liberation. Perhaps the clearest indication of this is the number of heterosexual people who play an active role in the community. Often it has been said that if sexual orientation were our only concern, there would be no room for straight people to join with us. However, in actuality, heterosexual persons are among the most active and outspoken members of Spirit of the Mountains. One heterosexual, married woman told me that she felt more comfortable raising her concerns about violence against women in this setting than in her previous church experience. She believed that her concerns would be heard, and that the connections between sexism, heterosexism, and violence would be understood and acted upon as part of the commitment to creating a just peace community.

One cannot work toward a vision of sexual justice without returning to the root causes and origins of homophobia, which have to do with power and control. As we work together in acts of solidarity and love, we know the Spirit of the Holy One in our midst, drawing us together. Inclusivity, connectedness, and making connections are key components to the work and theology of liberation for lesbian/gay/bisexual persons in any setting.

Heyward's fourth lesson is that "It is our responsibility to discern together what is good and what is evil in our own praxis."[12] One of the statements I hear repeatedly from lesbian/gay/bisexual persons as they begin to come out and claim the sacredness of their own personhood is: "They lied to me. What they said is not true." The reference here may be to parents, teachers, pastors, peers, political leaders, musicians, publishers, producers, or anyone else who has given the message that to be gay/lesbian/bisexual is to be sick, alone, unhappy, and bad. Certainly, in the act of claiming one's gay/lesbian/bisexual orientation, one must face grief and loss. However, this loss does not have anything to do with sexual orientation. Rather, one must grieve the losses enforced by the power of heterosexism and homophobia. Every gay/lesbian/bisexual person in this society must grieve multiple losses from the right to marry to the loss of safety/security. In addition, many of us must grieve the loss of relationships with family and friends.

Therefore, in the act of creating and articulating the process of liberation, it is imperative that lesbian/gay/bisexual persons speak for ourselves about what is good, healing, and holy. At the same time, we must also define what is and can be evil or oppressive within ourselves and our communities. Heyward observes: "In Nicaragua, it is not whether something can be labeled Christian or communist which makes it good or evil. It is whether it is liberating, life-affirming, sustaining, and empowering, or whether it is dominating, death-dealing, disrespectful, and destructive."[13]

There is a profound, nationwide movement working toward justice for lesbian/gay/bisexual persons that finds the source of its energy in people who may or may not have any formal or communal religious affiliation. Often these movements happen in spite of the prevailing religious attitudes. Even in a state as rural and small as New Hampshire, one can call the "Gay Info Line" to obtain information about support groups, study groups, advocacy groups, and political action groups. Within this praxis of organizing with others to bring about social change, lesbian/gay/bisexual persons discern what is good and evil, sacred and profane.

In conclusion, it becomes clear that the images of the church set forth in chapter 4, "A Liberating Theology of the Church," are images and metaphors of a faith community working toward liberation. It is also clear and significant that if one's theology and spirituality are liberating, they will be entwined with a psychology of liberation, establishing a healthier sense of self in relation to the community. Psychology and spirituality are deeply interwoven and need to be addressed as such in the community of faith.

The church/community of liberation is first and foremost the community called and led to leave behind social, political, and spiritual oppression and enslavement, and to create justice for all of God's people. Then and only then will its worship be a true celebration of the healing and hope-filled vision and power of God.

The church/community of liberation is the exiled community, placed outside of the powers and principalities of this world.

Only from this position can one be in solidarity with the many oppressed peoples who live under the control and power of the patriarchy.

The church/community of liberation is the incarnation of the body of Christ. Only through the embodiment and celebration of our body-selves can we begin to address the realities of people's lives with any integrity, relevancy, or redemption.

The hope that can take root and grow within these images of the church and the community of liberation is what compels many of us to continue to "come out while staying in," rather than to come out and leave. Perhaps one day the church will become what it is called to be. Perhaps it will become the community of liberation, committed to the specific struggle for justice of lesbian/gay/bisexual persons and all of God's children victimized by patriarchal control and domination. Perhaps it will be the community that supports the creation of healthy selves rather than fragmented and victimized emotionalities. Perhaps it will become the prophetic and constructive body of Christ, an agent of healing and transformation. In the meantime, many gay/lesbian/bisexual persons are dying emotionally, relationally, spiritually, economically, and physically. Therefore, in the words of one Spirit of the Mountains member, "In the meantime, we will continue to take care of ourselves."

Questions for Discussion

1. Who does the work of theology in your church community?

2. Who/what has influenced your own understanding of theology (as a child, as an adult)?

3. If you are gay/lesbian/bisexual, has your own theology helped or hindered your coming-out process?

4. Is our theology connected and relevant to your day-to-day life?

5. What is the connection between your own theology and the making of justice for gay/lesbian/bisexual persons?

6. How can your congregation help gay/lesbian/bisexual persons heal from internalized theological and psychological shame?

7. What does your church need to do to facilitate the building of a community of equals among gay, lesbian, bisexual, and heterosexual persons?

8. In your opinion, what would mainline churches need to do to put congregations like Spirit of the Mountains "out of business"?

9. What steps can your congregation take to become a community of liberation? How can your church "come out" as a liberation church?

6···

Stories of Hurting, Stories of Healing: Lesbian, Gay, and Bisexual Persons Speak of Their Experiences in the Church

As we saw in chapter 5, the significance and validity of any theology of liberation comes from its grounding in the real struggles of real people trying to live their lives within the context of an oppressive culture and/or society. Liberation theology is not simply an academic endeavor, born of books and intellectual discourse. Rather, it is the fruition of the praxis of God's people as we act and reflect on our journeys toward wholeness. In addition to the theological importance of this action and reflection, the praxis of liberation theology is closely intertwined with the journey toward psychological wholeness and health. When persons reflect theologically on the realities of their lives as they actually live them, rather than on the projections of others, then externalizaton of those projections can occur and psychological integration is possible. In other words, a theology of liberation leads to a psychology of liberation.

The purpose of this chapter is to weave concrete life experience into the theological and psychological frameworks. The interconnectedness of psychological and theological/spiritual experiences and reflections will be revealed in individual interviews. Throughout individual comments, one can hear the significant relationship between psychological and theological/ spiritual liberation.

Context of the Survey

In this chapter, lesbian, gay, bisexual, and heterosexual people related to the United Church of Christ speak about their own lives and experiences of homophobia and heterosexism in the church. This "telling the story" will happen in two ways. Primarily, I will relate the results of fifteen in-depth interviews, which I held during 1993. Each of these interviews was held individually and confidentially, usually lasting about one hour. The interview questions may be found in appendix A. Secondarily, I will refer to three other recent studies that interface with my own work. I hope that through this process the reader may gain a sense of the depths of pain, as well as the power and promise of healing, within and on the margin of the community of faith.

Although much of this information is relevant to all religious communities and denominations, it is important to understand both the larger and more immediate contexts, the systems within which this study is undertaken. Christopher Carrington states that "As a denomination, the United Church of Christ developed one of the most elaborate and progressive records of addressing issues of sexual and affectional orientation."[1] Much of this, he claims is due to a combination of factors related to both structure and values.

> The structural context of First Church including the democratic polity of the UCC, the association of UCC churches with institutions of higher education, the connection of UCC members to social movement organizations, enabled extensive negotiations. . . . The official affirmation and inclusion of lesbian and gay people most often occurs in churches with democratic governance (e.g. the United Church of Christ, the Unitarian-Universalists, the Quakers, the Metropolitan Community Church).[2]

The United Church of Christ has a longer history than most liberal Protestant denominations of addressing the concerns of lesbian/gay/bisexual persons as well as dealing with the injustices of homophobia and heterosexism. At the same time, however, organizations such as the Biblical Witness Fellowship become stronger, working to prevent the ordination and call of lesbian/gay/bisexual clergy and prevent the growth of the Open and Affirming (ONA) movement. Because of the church's congregational polity, each congregation is autonomous, electing its lay leadership, calling its pastors, writing and adopting its own by-laws, collecting its own financial resources, and owning its own property. Therefore, the General Synod cannot declare that congregations must become ONA, it can only encourage them. As I learned in my UCC polity class in seminary, "The General Synod does not speak for the churches, but to the churches."

As a result of this congregational polity and democratic decision-making process, there can be great discrepancies between the national policies, as set by General Synod, and those of the local churches, as well as vast differences from congregation to congregation. Therefore, these differing messages given by different parts of the system can produce in the individual a cognitive and emotional dissonance and a psychological double-bind. For example, it is possible to be a member of a denomination that officially affirms the ordination of lesbian/gay/ bisexual ministers and even to walk with the denomination's president in the March on Washington for gay/lesbian/bisexual/transgender rights while still belonging to a local church that refuses to call (or even fires) an openly lesbian or gay pastor and regularly engages in heterosexist and homophobic practices and policies. Therefore, even though the denomination is one of the most progressive in the work for sexual justice, the individual's experience within it may be a very different story of isolation and oppression.

This dynamic of the vast chasm between denominational policy and local church experience can have significant effects on the psychological and theological/spiritual experience of lesbian/gay/ bisexual persons. The mixed message about potential roles, relationships, and positions in the system often results in a very confusing and disturbing experience. For example, it has been a fairly common occurrence for lesbian/gay/bisexual persons who experience a vocational call to ordained ministry to transfer from other denominations to the UCC because of the national policy. Four out of seven clergypersons interviewed for this study relate having made this choice for this reason. Each of these four have expressed feeling disappointed, confused, and frustrated by the discrepancy between their denominational and local church experiences.

In order to understand fully the psychological impact of this experience, one can refer again to the importance of the system and the power of internalized messages in the experience of the self. In order to leave a system, such as the church of one's childhood, one must face significant emotional loss. One is walking away from the community in which one grew and was affirmed and confirmed as a child of God. As we saw in chapter 3, the church often understands and describes itself in terms of family relationships. Therefore, the experience of psychological attachment—especially to the church of one's family of origin—is very deep, on both conscious and unconscious levels. All four clergy members who related changing denominations described feeling anxious, alone, sad, and even guilty for having made this choice. Nonetheless, the anticipation of a new church "family," a new system that would fully include them, was motivation to make this transition. However, when the new system seemed to replicate the old system, the individuals were once again thrown into psychological and theological distress.

I believe that under these circumstances, the experience of shame goes even further underground and perhaps becomes unconscious in the psyche, its internalization making it even more insidious. Presumably, an individual has gone through the process of understanding the messages of shame projected onto him/her by different persons and positions in the system, as well as by the homophobia interwoven into the system itself. Then the person has name these messages for what they are and stepped out of the field of projection, presumably with the support of some kind of self-affirming subsystem. Next, after having made the decision to trust the messages of another system, he or she begins to experience similar silencing, rejection, projection, and projective identification. Once again, the lesbian/gay/bisexual person experiences victimization by the sexually dysfunctional denominational system. Obviously, this process could reactivate those previously internalized messages that the individual had chosen to leave behind, and possibly place the new positive sense of self in relation to others in jeopardy all over again. Perhaps at some point, the lesbian/gay/bisexual person who has had this experience might integrate the previously split images of good and bad, as he/she had projected them onto competing denominations/church families (e.g., *this* church is all good; *that* church is all bad). However, the destructive power of the internalization of shame and the double bind far overshadow this possible integration that would occur more appropriately in the development of a healthy self-in-relation.

Theologically and spiritually, this repetitive experience of being disenfranchised and excluded reinforces the sense of alienation from the body of Christ, compromising the integrity of the community called to lead the people from bondage. As one clergyperson, who had been ordained as a catholic priest, stated in his interview, "My religious community has as a cornerstone a solid identification with the disenfranchised, but to be a part of them I have to keep quiet about my own disenfranchisement." Again, one identifies with the Christ outside the city gate of Jerusalem, exiled from one's own community of faith.

Interview Results

The interviews related in this chapter are important because they speak of the real-life experience out of which liberating theology and psychology emerge. During 1993 and 1994, I held in-depth interviews with fifteen individuals (see interview questions in appendix B), each of whom spoke very openly about his or her own experiences of the church, religion, homophobia, and liberation. All of these people live in New England, and have had some level of connection with Spirit of the Mountains worshiping community. Some may have only attended once or twice, while others have been present for almost every event since its beginning. The results of this survey are in no way meant to be empirical data to prove a hypothesis. Nonetheless, within these interviews, one can sense a pattern of responses I believe is not unique to these fifteen individuals. In fact, some significant similarities exist between the results of these interviews and other surveys that will be mentioned.

The fifteen people interviewed included seven lesbians, four gay men, two bisexuals, one heterosexual, and one who stated,

"I haven't thought about any category for myself." Seven are ordained clergy (six UCC and one Catholic), one is "in care" for ordination in the UCC, and seven are lay persons. Only three of the fifteen grew up in the UCC, while ten have transferred to the UCC (five stated that this was due to the UCC policy regarding gay/lesbian/bisexual persons, mostly in respect to the ONA movement and UCC policy on ordination), and two are related to the UCC only through their participation in Spirit of the Mountains.

One respondent was not active in religion until adulthood. Two, as children, attended church on their own, without their families. Four were raised Catholic, one was raised in an Assembly of God congregation, two were raised by their families in the UCC, and six were raised in other Protestant churches.

At present, all fifteen participate in Spirit of the Mountains. In addition, two are United Church of Christ pastors, three are members of UCC churches and do supply preaching, and one serves as a UCC interim pastor. Two stated that currently they are members of UCC churches but are not active; two others are active members of UCC churches, one of which is an ONA congregation. One person stated that she participates monthly in a Quaker meeting, and one continues to have an official relationship with the Catholic Church.

When asked how they currently describe themselves religiously, responses were varied. Nine described themselves as "Christian"; however, two qualified their responses, saying: "I'm afraid to say this word due to the fundamentalist association with it—so I'm also creation-centered," and "I'm Christian, but not exclusively so." Four described themselves as "feminist-Christian. One described herself as "post-Christian," while another described herself as "Judeo-Christian."

Everyone responded that he/she has had several experiences of homophobia/heterosexism in the church. In some of these experiences, the person him/herself was the target of the homophobic or heterosexist action, and in some, they witnessed others being victimized. Some of these experiences consisted of overhearing homophobic statements (one person stated that he sat through a church dinner during which the conversation was punctuated with "gay jokes"). Still other experiences consisted of silence around the issue of homosexuality, and the resulting internalization of the belief that it is not okay to raise this concern in church.

Question: Have you experienced homophobia or heterosexism in the church? If so, please describe one or two of these experiences.

Response: "It was very painful to not be able to get married in the church where I had my membership. I had to go to the UUA (Unitarian-Universalist Association) to feel safe—so that I would not be 'outed' and risk my job, and would feel accepted and affirmed" (clergy).

Response: "When my partner and I had our seventh anniversary, I wanted to place flowers on the altar. In our church, married couples who celebrate anniversaries give the altar flowers, and their anniversary is noted in the bulletin. Even though we had been going through an Open and Affirming study, I couldn't speak up. I never asked, because I was afraid. I didn't want to raise conflict and have it come back at me. So it never happened, and that makes me sad" (laity).

Response: "The most painful moment I remember was a confrontation with my mother who is very active in church. She said to me, 'Are you gay? Because if you are, I will simply take a gun to your head and put you out of your misery'" (clergy).

Response: "Overhearing things like, 'Sure we welcome homosexuals like we welcome prostitutes and anybody, but not as church leaders and certainly not as pastors'" (clergy).

Response: "Looking for a new church after my divorce. The first thing they asked was 'Are you married? Do you have kids?' It was like they were asking, 'Do you fit the mold?' I longed to be part of a church family, and realized that I had to suppress my real self and pretend to fit in" (laity).

Response: "It was most hurtful that I know that people wanted me out of the church because I was a lesbian, but wouldn't say it directly. Instead they made up things about my work and devalued it, turning what was good into something bad." (clergy).

Response: "There was too much hypocrisy. People were organizing to get our lesbian minister to resign. They were saying one thing to my face and then another, so I couldn't confront the homophobia. Don't lie to me and say that sexuality was never the issue—bullshit!" (laity).

(These two preceding responses were from persons who had been in different parishes.)

Response: "I haven't been in church until coming to Spirit of the Mountains. I didn't feel worthy, acceptable, or accepted by the church" (laity).

Response: "What hurts is people with self-righteous attitudes about the Bible who condemn me with it, but they don't do it with other issues" (clergy).

Response: "There is pain in trying to get rid of my own internalized homophobia so that I can be strong enough to confront the church" (laity).

Response: "It hurts when people say things like, 'This issue threatens to blow apart the church,' or 'If we drop this, more people will come to church.' We dropped it and no one came" (laity).

Response: "I didn't leave the church because of the bigots. I left because of the so-called liberals who did nothing. I got the message that the institution was more important than the mission" (laity).

Perhaps more profoundly than any theological statement can explain, these comments express the experience of feeling exiled, outside of the gate to the community of faith. Over and over again, people described their experiences, beliefs, and feelings that to come out, and give voice to the real self, means to somehow lose the community of faith. Therefore, we are faced with the choice of alienation from self or alienation from the church. Because we experience God in the *community* of faith, some aspects of our relationship with God are compromised in this experience of exile. Because we gain much of our sense of self through relationship, unless we make the transition to a new, more empowering community of faith, some of our self is also compromised in the experience of exile. Even then, we must face the psychological pain and anxiety of rejection, and the spiritual shame of rejection.

Question: Have you experienced any moments of healing in regard to homophobia or heterosexism in the church? If so, please describe.

Response: "Probably Spirit of the Mountains is the most healing—the acceptance and not being labeled here—we are one in the things that count. I don't feel estranged" (laity).

Response: "The March on Washington was healing, especially being in the church service—the size, the sound, the warmth, and it wasn't all gay and lesbian people" (laity).

Response: "The covenant service of my friends this summer—strong women who know their worth and value. They were able to make a commitment. I was overawed, like the awe you feel for God and all-encompassing love" (laity).

Response: "The UCC national and conference proactive positions keep me here" (clergy).

Response: "I have known affirmation by individuals, but in regard to the church, I can't think of anything healing. The church at large continues to disappoint me" (clergy).

Response: "Healing comes in renegade forms, outside of the mainline definition of 'church,' like when I was at a women's concert and heard another lesbian say, 'I am made in God's image'" (clergy).

Response: "It is healing to network with other gay/lesbian/bisexual people who call themselves Christian" (clergy).

Response: "Joining an ONA church as a couple was healing" (laity).

Response: "My own individual faith has been stronger than the church's homophobia. I never felt abandoned by God when I was abandoned by the church" (laity).

Response: "It is healing to tell my story. I have come out to friends, and they have changed and become advocates, champions. Decent people get transformed by hearing our stories" (clergy).

Response: "It was monumental to watch another lesbian pastor come out at annual meeting. A church member put her arm around me. She knew what it meant to me" (clergy).

Response: "Spirit of the Mountains has been healing. I belong there as I never did in a traditional church. I feel accepted there and don't have to work at it" (laity).

Again, this sampling of answers to the question profoundly speaks to the theological and psychological issues raised in this book. In regard to the theology and spirituality raised in these statements, two points emerge as significant. Specifically, in the liberation action/reflection model of praxis, lesbian/gay/bisexual persons create a theology that is healing and relevant to our lives. Repeatedly, persons spoke of the influence of activism on their theology and spirituality. Related to this is the significance of relationships, especially the experience of an accepting and affirming community.

In regard to the psychological experience as intertwined with the experience of faith, one cannot help but notice the importance of the self-in-relation to others as foundational to the psychological health of lesbian/gay/bisexual persons. As people spoke of being in community that was affirming of the sexual self and active in its advocacy, they spoke in imagery and words descriptive of increased self-esteem, psychological congruence, and emotional health.

Question: If you could say anything to "the church" in regard to homophobia and heterosexism, what would you say?

Response: "My conflict is not about my faith or my relationship to God, only about my relationship to the church" (clergy).

Response: "When I came out to myself, I became more spiritually connected than ever before" (clergy).

Response: "Don't be silent. Being gay is an option that must be talked about by the church, especially in small towns" (laity).

Response: "This is who I am. I cannot change. What do you expect of me? To repent or live a life of loneliness that you are not willing to live? As you set aside gay and lesbian people, you are saying that for at least 10 percent of the world's population, Christianity has nothing to say" (clergy).

Response: "I'm really sorry there isn't room for me to be a minister in the church—for my own emotional, theological, and physical health I had to move out. I know it hurts me. I don't think the church knows that it is hurt" (clergy).

Response: "An older couple handed me a letter on my last day at the church. It stated, 'We liked you as our pastor. Our daughter is a lesbian.' These people don't have a safe place in the church" (clergy).

Response: "I feel like a target. But if homosexuals weren't the target, someone else would be. We must find the roots of oppression. There's a spiritual issue here—What's missing that is being filled by oppression?" (laity).

Response: "I guess I have some hope, stupidly so. Enough individuals are coming to consciousness about this that the church will either have to deal with it or die" (clergy).

Response: "It's all been said. You can say it one hundred more times. It's not a matter of getting people to listen. It's getting people to be courageous enough to act on their beliefs. If the people who believe that homophobia is wrong would speak up, it would change" (laity).

Response: "We're here. We're not going away. It's like that prayer during the time of the Nazis. If you're going to point the finger and exclude, there will be no one left for you. Stop closing your eyes out of fear. No amount of putting people into concentration camps will make us go away" (clergy).

Reflections

Although each of these comments is unique and personal, some common themes are interwoven throughout the statements. Many responses recounted painful moments and experiences. Many persons have had to deal with the loss of position, power, relationship, and even safety upon coming out in the church. In addition, respondents related significant hurt and alienation from times of feeling prejudged and objectified.

As one might suspect, the nature of hopeful and healing moments is conversely related to this kind of pain. Specifically, the times that people described as healing and hopeful seem to cluster around two experiences. First is the experience of telling and hearing our stories: To speak and be heard is a powerful moment. People who have been closeted, pretending to live out one story, when in fact the real story is very different, know the power of "hearing one another to speech," as was stated once by Nelle Morton, a feminist Christian theologian.[3] It is faithful, it is spiritual, it is Christian to "love to tell the story." I know from my own experience that when I came out publicly in a church sanctuary in the presence of hundreds of church members, I felt the burdens of secretiveness taken up into the rafters, and I experienced a powerful spiritual rebirth.

Second, many characterized coming together in community as a healing experience. Respondents regularly cited the hopeful experience of being accepted and active in a community that works for justice and inclusivity. It is interesting to note that two of the people who stated that they find acceptance for who they are as critical to their healing are primarily heterosexual (one is self-named, while the other does not think of herself in "categories" but is in a heterosexual marriage).

Finally, it was stated in the responses to the last question as well as throughout other questions that persons continue to experience dissonance between the institution of the church and their own faith. Therefore, when offered the chance to say anything to the church, persons were able to do so with some level of self-esteem and differentiation.

In 1991 and 1992, Gary David Comstock conducted a survey of 289 gay and lesbian persons in the United Church of Christ and 189 in the United Methodist Church. One of the conclusions from this survey is reported in *Gay Theology without Apology*:

> Working on human needs and bringing people together tend to be our common practice. Three-quarters of both lay and clergy respondents report active involvement in ministry outside of their respective denomination, most often in the form of AIDS advocacy and services, volunteer counseling, lesbian/gay support services and activism, hunger and homeless projects, community services, social justice advocacy, interfaith events and organizations, women's antiviolence projects, and youth programs.[4]

This seems similar, although it is not identical, to some of the experiences related throughout the interviews I conducted. In these interviews, people stated that they often found healing moments in those communities where people gathered to work for justice and inclusivity for lesbian/gay/bisexual persons. The results of Comstock's work and my own suggest that the combination of community, advocacy for justice, and inclusivity are key ingredients to a gay/lesbian/bisexual theology, spirituality, and psychology of liberation, as well as to the work of all Christian sexual ethics.

In "Yours in Sisterhood: A Lesbian and Bisexual Perspective on Ministry," Deborah H. Carney and Susan E. Davies survey lesbian and bisexual women in the church. The researchers report that the respondents (ten women) relate having experienced significant oppression within the church. After discussing participants' responses to questions about internalized homophobia, difficulties on relationships, conflicts between lifestyle and vows, and other questions of importance, the authors conclude the following:

> The ten women . . . have a vision that sustains them. It is a vision of a church and a world in which belonging and identity will not be dependent on one's sexual orientation or cultural status, but rather on the pluralistic, progressive spirit of Jesus Christ. . . .

Each finds herself in the classic dilemma of having received a vision of wholeness and health, justice and shalom, from the very institution that denies both the embodiment of that vision and often her very right to exist. And yet they stay, at least for the time being, determined to evangelize the church they love with "patience and grace and blessed unrest."[5]

Again this survey and article confirm a significant issue that was raised repeatedly in the interviews for this book. Over and over again, people declared that their experience of God's love and the church's institutionalization of that love are two separate and distinct experiences. As one respondent at Spirit of the Mountains said, "I have never felt abandoned by God, only by the church."

In 1993, I received a Christmas card from a gay couple, both of whom are clergy and had been seeking a call to a church for more than a year. Their note clearly states the distinction between the love of God and the institution of the church: "We need to get on with our lives, and realize that if the rules of the institutional church do not include us, we need not wring our hands helplessly, but instead need to change the game and write rules grounded in visions of the realized kingdom of God, not in fear and misunderstanding."[6] Since then, they have received a call and are serving as co-associate pastors of the University Christian Church in Seattle, Washington.

Even though several theological and psychological themes have been raised throughout this chapter, I believe it is important to reiterate a few key points. First, as is congruent throughout the body of this writing, the examples of interview statements convey the intricate and intimate relationship of psychological and theological realities of lesbian/gay/bisexual persons. Indeed, a theology/spirituality of liberation leads to a psychology of liberation. Experiences of theological wholeness are the same experiences that lead to psychological health. The member of the body of Christ and the self-in-relation are two different lenses through which one views and interprets the same experience.

One cannot isolate the individual psychologically or theologically from the system or community of faith. Who we understand ourselves to be, as children of God and as whole human beings, is significantly molded by our interactions with others and the surrounding environment. On the one hand, this can lead to isolation and oppression; on the other hand, it can lead to liberation and true community. "The March on Washington was healing—especially being in the church service—the size, the sounds, the warmth."

Within the system of the church (the United Church of Christ and the Christian church at large), lesbian/gay/bisexual persons function as objects of projection and projective identification. As one person asked, "What is missing in people's experience that is somehow filled by oppression?" Lesbian/gay/bisexual persons interviewed expressed their sense of being targets of other people's shame, fear, and violence. "If you are [gay], then I will simply take a gun to your head and put you out of your misery." Sometimes, lesbian/gay/bisexual persons describe the experience of being caught in projective identification by internalizing the shame and lack of self-worth. "I didn't feel worthy or acceptable to walk inside a church door."

Lesbian/gay/bisexual persons speak about the need to create psychological subsystems/theological communities that strengthen the sense of self and spirit. This is a primary way of exorcising and externalizing toxic shame. "Spirit of the Mountains—it's peaceful. . . . I can bring my sexual orientation into worship."

When lesbian/gay/bisexual and heterosexual persons create community together, then we can heal the experience of splitting (good vs. bad, gay vs. straight) that occurs individually and systemically. Splitting and projection are not functions of sexual orientation, but of being human. Therefore, in an inclusive community, we stand a better chance to withdraw our psychological projections and theological dualisms. "Spirit of the Mountains is the most healing—we are one in the things that count."

Sexuality and spirituality are intimately connected. In various ways, several respondents related that they cannot leave their sexual orientation at the door of the church and pick up their spiritual orientation for worship. Sexuality is an integral part of the self, and createdness is an integral part of who we are as children of God. The liturgical celebration of our sexuality is a profoundly healing experience. "The covenant service of my friends. . . . I was overawed, like the awe you feel for God."

Despite the significant pain, loss, frustration, and alienation expressed by the lesbian/gay/bisexual persons interviewed, their relationship with the church continues to be important. Perhaps this significance is due to the system's power and influence on the self. Perhaps it is due to lesbian/gay/bisexual persons' lack of differentiation from the oppressive object of shame. Certainly, these issues may be a part of this relationship. However, it may also be the result of the spiritual grounding found in the eschatology and prophecy of the people called. The church, as the embodiment of the Christ, is called out of bondage to move toward the promised land of liberation. Lesbian/gay/bisexual Christians, finding healing in the liberating love of God and the vision of the just reign of God, become an empowered and powerful presence, even in the face of all that would stop us. "If the rules of the institutional church do not include us, we need not wring our hands helplessly, but instead need to change the game and write rules grounded in visions of the realized kingdom of God, not in fear and misunderstanding."[7]

Questions for Discussion

1. What was it like to listen to some of the stories and reflections of the people in this chapter? What surprised you? What saddened you? What gave you hope?

2. How have you experienced homophobia/heterosexism in the church?

3. What story would you add to this chapter?

4. If you could say anything to the church regarding homophobia and heterosexism, what would it be?

5. How are the key ingredients of the gay/lesbian/bisexual theology of liberation (community, advocacy for justice, inclusivity) present in your own faith life? In the life of your congregation?

7 · · ·

Conclusions, Implications, and Suggestions for Ministry

Now more than ever there is an urgent need to address the concerns of gay/lesbian/bisexual persons in the church and society. Since the Stonewall riot in 1969, gay/lesbian/bisexual activists and our supporters have become more and more visible and organized. However, we pale in comparison to those who oppose us. In the recent past, the political, economic, and social power of the religious and secular right has increased dramatically, and is moving from the margins to the mainstream of political and legal power and process. This powerful presence has been manifest nationally in the 1994 elections, in the administration's compromised military policy of "Don't ask, don't tell," and in the amount of publicity given to extremists like Ralph Reed (the director of the Christian Coalition). On a more local level, the power of the right is evidenced in the rapidly increasing number of state and local antigay legislative initiatives being introduced across our country and in the organized efforts to gain majorities on local school boards and city councils.

Twice this week, I read newspaper reports concerning the increasing strength of the religious right. First, an article in a local paper cited incidents at an area high school in Merrimack County, New Hampshire, where the religious right has been very active. A few months ago, they fired a teacher who had used books that included gay or lesbian characters. More recently, a policy was enacted to prevent same-sex persons from touching each other on school grounds. The article reported several incidents of friends hugging or touching each other to say goodbye or offer support. They were immediately reprimanded by school authorities for having violated the school's policy of intolerance toward anything that might support/promote homosexuality.

A few days later, I was reading an area religion page, when my eye was caught by a very large (and expensive) advertisement of the Traditional Values Coalition. Readers were being encouraged to come hear the Reverend Louis P. Sheldon (a national leader in the religious right movement) speak about "the right to life, homosexuality, pornography, the family, religious liberty, and what you can do." I feel sure that the church will be filled to capacity when he speaks.

> Any review of the history of the religious and secular right in our country reveals that this wing is after cultural and political supremacy. . . . At its core, this right-wing movement rejects the two-hundred-year-old experiment of American pluralism and, in its place, proposes a Christian state, a theocracy. Right-wing leaders and organizations explicitly reject democratic values like tolerance, dissent, individual freedom, and compromise. Indeed, the right elevates intolerance to a virtue if it is based on Christian values.[1]

We cannot afford to ignore the power or goals of this movement. If we do, there likely will be severe consequences—not only for gay/lesbian/bisexual persons, but also for gay and straight people of color, women, children, and others.

I am reminded of a button that I received at a Gay/lesbian Pride March several years ago. The background is a pink triangle (the sign worn by gay men in Nazi concentration camps), and it features a saying attributed to Pastor Martin Niemolier, a Protestant minister in Nazi Germany. It reads:

> In Germany they first came for the Communists, and I didn't speak up because I wasn't a Communist. Then they came for the Jews, and I didn't speak up because I wasn't Jewish. Then they came for the trade unionists, and I didn't speak up because I wasn't a trade unionist. Then they came for the Catholics, and I didn't speak up because I was a Protestant. Then, they came for me—and by that time no one was left to speak up.[2]

This is not to suggest that all individuals who follow the religious right are bad. However, it is poignant that the right appeals to many who feel politically and economically powerless (or extremely powerful) and overwhelmed. The similarities to the Nazi party's appeal to the Germans during Hitler's rise are frightening.

> That ordinary, peace-loving, deeply faithful people follow the religious right does not disguise the truth that its leaders have organized a militantly antidemocratic movement. . . . The enemy is not religion, God, the Spirit, or people of faith. The enemy is evil. Prejudice, injustice, inequality, intolerance, hatred, violence are all evils being strengthened by the religious and supremist right.[3]

On behalf of gays, lesbians, and bisexuals and all persons everywhere, each congregation needs to become active in the work of advocacy and justice. Since so much of the hostility toward lesbian/gay/bisexual people is rooted in religion, we cannot afford to be uninvolved or complacent.

It is hoped that through the material presented in this book, the reader will have gained a keener sense of the experience of lesbian/gay/bisexual persons within the United Church of Christ in particular and across mainstream churches in general. Of particular importance is the interweaving of the psychological, theological, and spiritual experiences of lesbian/gay/bisexual persons who seek to remain within the structure of a denomination that presents mixed messages about sexual justice and the place of lesbians/gays/bisexuals in the church. By presenting direct quotations from persons who were interviewed, I have attempted to provide heterosexual readers with the opportunity to *feel* and identify emotionally what it is like for lesbian/gay/bisexual persons in the church. In addition, I hope that lesbian/gay/bisexual readers have found some sense of shared experience and community here.

As a lesbian who has engaged in educational efforts in the church for years, I know that being understood intellectually and being empathized with emotionally are two very different experiences. I have heard others verbalize my own reactions of frustration, anger, and pain at being considered as an "issue" to be debated, rather than a person to be known. To really listen to the individual stories of lesbian, gay, bisexual and heterosexual persons as we struggle in our relationships with the church is to begin to know one another as people and not as depersonalized issues. It is difficult, if not impossible, to depersonalize homophobia when one hears the story of a minister whose mother, an active church member, told him, "If you're gay I might as well shoot you to put you out of your misery." This is important to remember when engaging in any kind of ministry concerning the lives of lesbian/gay/bisexual persons. We are not an issue. We are people. We need to be listened to and known as people.

It is my belief that one of the most significant steps the church can take in this journey toward liberation is that of listening. So often we assert that the call of the church is to preach the good news. In regard to the issues of sexual justice, perhaps the church has preached too much and listened too little. Any place within the system is an appropriate entry for the voices of lesbian/gay/bisexual persons. This sacred act of listening can occur in women's and men's communal groups and small-group studies, as significantly as it can occur at General Synod. Listening inevitably means the personalizing of issues and positions, and therefore, it makes possible the withdrawal of projections and objectifications that is necessary for psychological and social change and healing. The religious right knows this. Its leaders are preaching and teaching lies about gay/lesbian/bisexual persons, and people are believing them. People need to hear the truth and realities of gay/lesbian/bisexual persons of faith to counteract this campaign against us.

It is hoped that this book has given the reader a keener sense of the struggles of lesbian/gay/bisexual persons and a clearer understanding of homophobia and heterosexism and their place and power within the church and society. Homophobic beliefs, practices, and policies are interwoven into and undergird much of the life of the institutional church. Whether the beliefs give rise to the practices and policies, or the practices and policies give rise to the beliefs, is something of a chicken-and-egg question. For example, people may believe that it is appropriate to have a lesbian/gay/bisexual person as a member of their local church but not as its pastor. Perhaps they believe this because they are not aware of having ever known a lesbian/gay/bisexual pastor. Perhaps their present pastor, whom they regard highly, is a closeted lesbian/gay/bisexual person afraid to come out. If that church has never addressed the issues of homophobia or heterosexism, the pastor may be afraid of being fired or forced to resign, as has happened to other lesbian/gay/bisexual pastors. Thus, the realities of lesbian/gay/bisexual persons continue to be silenced, while the homophobic and heterosexist practices go unchallenged and the beliefs of church members remain unchanged. Homophobia and heterosexism create a vicious cycle of fear, silence, ignorance, and oppression within the life of the church.

This cycle will remain unchallenged and unchanged as long as people remain silent. Raising the concerns of lesbian/gay/bisexual persons and the issues of homophobia and heterosexism is the only way change will occur. As a slogan from the AIDS education campaign so aptly puts it, "silence equals death." Although breaking the silence around the issues of homophobia and heterosexism is critical, I do not mean to imply that it easy for churches to accomplish. As related in previous chapters, I believe that there are numerous intrapsychic, relational, and systemic factors that collude in maintaining the silence. Change is threatening. Systems of all kinds seek to maintain equilibrium and homeostasis. Therefore, one must be willing to confront the social, psychological, and theological forces that work to maintain the status quo. In the church, this often happens through the efforts of individuals or small groups, speaking up from their particular positions and experiences and risking reactions from others. According to structural family therapy, systems become dysfunctional when they become rigid in their responses. Therefore, the processes of change and movement occur when alternatives are presented, attempted, and become internalized into the structure of the system. This must happen in order for any real change to occur regarding the issues of homophobia and heterosexism within the church.

One important aspect of giving voice to the concerns of lesbian/gay/bisexual persons and addressing the power of homophobia and heterosexism is the identity of those who begin to speak. In some of the educational work I have done in local churches, I have heard the assumption that "There are no gay people here," or "If we do have gay people, they seem perfectly happy." First, one must assume that there are gay/lesbian/bisexual persons and their families everywhere, in every church, no matter how conservative or liberal. Before I came out publicly, I believed that I knew who was lesbian/gay/bisexual or had lesbian/gay/bisexual family members. In actuality I had no idea. After I came out and people began to talk more candidly with me, I began to realize that the number was much higher than I had ever imagined.

In systems theory, silence is understood as "negative feedback," meaning the absence of information and feedback. In the church, one cannot assume silence to mean that lesbian/gay/bisexual persons are absent, or that they are satisfied with things as they are. More likely, silence means fear of retaliation (lack of acceptance, gossip, job loss or difficulty at work because of church members who work in the same profession or business, etc.) or a level of internalized homophobia, shame, and scapegoating that will not allow persons to speak. This silence becomes the church's version of the military's oppressive "Don't ask, don't tell" policy.

To expect lesbian/gay/bisexual persons to be the ones to raise the concerns of homophobia and heterosexism is to miss significant factors. Specifically, homophobia is similar to racism, sexism, classism, and every other form of discrimination and prejudice. It not only affects those who are the direct object of the discrimination, it affects us all. I am becoming aware on a daily basis of how my own prejudices limit my understanding and knowledge not only of others but of myself. If I have a distorted image of others, then I have a distorted image of myself, of the community of God's people, and even of God. Psychologically speaking, I am inappropriately splitting good and bad objects, unconsciously projecting and objectifying others.

When I engage in beliefs and practices of discrimination, I overlook parts of myself as well as parts of the other. I inappropriately focus on how we are different rather than how we are the same. I have misconceptions about what it is to be human, and I cannot enter into full communion with God's people. Because I am afraid of true diversity, I prevent myself from knowing the fullness of God, in whose image each of us is created. At this point, neither psychology nor theology can be liberating, but only oppressive and dehumanizing.

As a white woman, I have learned that it is not the responsibility of people of color to address my racism any more than it is the responsibility of differently abled people to deal with my prejudice against them. It is my responsibility to deal with it. To expect people of color to educate me about my racism is to place an unfair burden on them and to displace my own responsibility. At the same time, to refuse to listen to them when they do speak and confront me with their experience of my community's racist beliefs, practices, and policies is to increase the power of racism and to further alienate the people of God. In the same vein, it is not the responsibility of the disabled person to build a wheelchair ramp into the church, but it is my responsibility as an able-bodied person to listen to what it is like to get into church with a wheelchair, and then to build a ramp.

It is not the responsibility of lesbian/gay/bisexual persons to raise the issue of homophobia in the church. It is neither fair nor realistic for heterosexual persons to expect gay/lesbian/bisexual persons to speak up about our lives or to assume that if we do not, it is because we are happy with the way things are. Whether or not one speaks the truth about one's life is a personal choice. As many of the interviewees affirmed, "telling our stories" is an act of sacred healing—not because it addresses the heterosexism of others, but because it is an act of radical self-acceptance and trust.

Yes, the issue must be raised in order to break the support, both silent and overt, for heterosexist practices. However, in order to remain faithful to the call of the Christian community, the victims of prejudice are not the ones who must raise the concerns. Rather it is the responsibility of anyone and everyone. Perhaps the UCC motto states it best: "That they may all be one."

In addition to affirming the call of the community of faith to speak up on behalf of the victim, it is important to note some of the previously mentioned concepts of systems theory that make it difficult, if not impossible, for those who are victimized to speak and be heard. If lesbian/gay/bisexual persons are placed in the position of the scapegoat, carrying the sexual shame for the institution, then it will be virtually impossible for us to speak and be heard with systemic authority and power. Scapegoats are objectified and not taken seriously. Projected shame also objectifies and, as it is internalized, prevents persons from speaking and hearing one another as valued children of God. Therefore, it is not the victims alone who will be able to speak and be heard. Rather, only through a combination of moves and countermoves, changes and reactions, interchanges and interactions will lesbian/gay/bisexual persons be enabled to speak and be heard within the institution.

The social and political leadership of the lesbian/gay/bisexual community is calling to and challenging individuals to come out publicly. If more of us did come out, then many false assumptions and stereotypes would be broken down and we would be more empowered to seek and create justice. I believe that it is the work of each parish to create support and safety so that gay/lesbian/bisexual persons in your church and community can come out within the context and protection of true community. If there is one sentence that captures the essence of this book, this is it: Gay/lesbian/bisexual people cannot be expected to do the work of the church alone. If we are to be faithful to the church, then we need the church to be faithful to us, and with us. Community is a sacred gift from God, but only by standing with each other, risking together, loving together, do we make it holy.

As much as we are called to be prophetic in vision and action, we must also be realistic in expectation. As was discussed in chapter 3, the church is a system, and all systems are motivated by the pull toward equilibrium. In other words, for every prophetic move toward change, there may be a regressive move to negate this change. Despite the intense power of systems—or perhaps because of it—it is critical to address homophobia and heterosexism with the larger picture in mind. Nevertheless, because of the interactional nature of systems, a change in any part of the system will effect changes throughout the system. Therefore, one cannot assume that changes in national policy do not affect the local church, even though the change often seems very slow. Neither should one assume that a change in a small parish within a small town does not affect national policy. In other words, wherever one is within the body of Christ, the institution of the church, there is important work to be done, with ramifications throughout the denomination. It is no accident that while ONA statements and nondiscrimination policies are being presented throughout the denomination, there is also an increase in discrimination and prejudice. This same principle is evident in society in the increasing visibility of gay/lesbian/bisexual people and the increasing number of antigay legislative efforts.

As much as homophobia and heterosexism seem to be interwoven into the fabric of the church, and as powerful as is homophobic prejudice within the church and society, I believe that oppression is not the last word. From a strictly systems perspective and in light of the confluence of homophobia in society, the denomination, and many local parishes, the hope for change is slight. On the other hand, some change is beginning to happen in some places; and therefore, change, ever so slight, is happening everywhere. As a person of faith, I use systems theory, object relations theory, and self-in-relation theory as tools for understanding the interactions within the institution but not as the final word of reality. The final word is God's call to us to leave our chains of bondage and move toward the vision of a just peace in the realm of God. It is God's call to us to create together a theology and spirituality of liberation that emerges out of the praxis of our day-to-day lives as we work to create communities of sexual justice and psychological well-being.

We in the church are bound together through our mutual covenant with God. We are called together to leave behind oppression and join in communal liturgy born of our journey toward freedom, the "holy land." We are saved together as we experience and are a part of the healing of creation through the work and worship of making peace with justice.

Perhaps the most profound embodiment of this understanding in the recent history of the United Church of Christ has occurred through the Open and Affirming (ONA) movement. "While not always easy, when done with care, an ONA process frequently deepens a church's spiritual life and sense of community."[4] As I have spoken with several persons who have engaged in ONA studies within their churches, there has been one overriding response: Engaging in the ONA study process has deepened the congregation's spiritual life and enabled them to search and struggle with their faithfulness as has no other issue. In 1993, the ONA program of the United Church of Christ for Lesbian/Gay Concerns (UCCL/GC) engaged in a study to gain an understanding of the experience of the ONA churches at that time. Sixty-four of the ninety-four churches responded. The study clearly indicated that engaging in this process enhances the faith and spirituality of the community. The report states: "It has deepened us spiritually and allowed us to be more 'risky' re. social justice. . . . We are seeking to live in compassionate ways and are trying to resist 'the system' with all its 'isms.' . . . ONA has deepened our faith commitment, financial giving, meant greater openness to theological growth, and increased sensitivity to inclusiveness issues."[5]

To address the discrimination of homophobia and heterosexism and to engage in the liberation of lesbian/gay/bisexual persons is to be faithful to the call and covenant of the church. Therefore, these are not processes that will ultimately divide, dehumanize, or destroy the church, even though they do raise significant conflict. They are processes that threaten much of the operative belief system, psychological and social projections, and projective identifications, theological images, and structures of authority and power through the institution. As a result, they often feel very risky and overwhelmingly scary for some. I imagine that the trip out of slavery in Egypt into the unknown of the wilderness also felt this way: "But the people thirsted for water, and complained against Moses and said, 'Why did you bring us out of Egypt to kill us and our children and livestock with thirst?' So Moses cried out to [God], 'What shall I do with these people? They are almost ready to stone me'" (Exod. 17:3–4).

No journey out of oppression toward liberation is easy. One does not know exactly what hungers, thirsts, and conflicts one will encounter along the way. In the midst of the wilderness, many of the Israelites expressed their feelings of anguish that the slavery they knew was better than the liberation they did not know. Despite the evidence of the presence and promise of God, people were afraid and despairing that nothing would get better.

In the book of Exodus, God led the Israelites along this journey through the person of Moses and fed them manna one day at a time. In the same way, God is leading the church today on a journey toward the liberation of lesbian/gay/bisexual persons. Like the Israelites, we do not know exactly what is ahead. We do not know exactly how difficult our journey will be or what will be sacrificed. We do know that each day we travel together brings the revitalizing of faith and deepening of spirit to individuals, congregations, and the denomination. We also know that to fail to engage in the liberation of lesbian/gay/bisexual persons, along with the liberation of all of God's children and creation, is to refuse to seek the vision and live within the covenant of our healing and loving God.

So what steps must we take now on this journey? As the interviewees indicated, there is an overarching need to speak the truth of our lives and be heard without fear of retaliation or rejection. In the Christian tradition of telling and retelling the story of faith, lesbian/gay/bisexual persons within the church need to do the same. Storytelling is an act of faith in which we engage all the time. How we celebrate worship, how we introduce ourselves to strangers, what we inscribe on our church signs tells the story of who we understand ourselves to be. Storytelling as an act of faith has been denied for too long to lesbian/gay/bisexual persons. Gay/lesbian/bisexual persons need to speak; heterosexual persons need to listen. Together we need to create a safe environment in which all persons feel respected and cherished as part of the body of Christ.

This kind of storytelling can happen in numerous ways. As an alternative to the Traditional Values Coalition advertisement, what if next week's paper held several invitations to the community to come and learn about the power of homophobia and listen to the life stories of gay/lesbian/bisexual Christians? This storytelling can also take place in small study and discussion groups, through guest preachers, etc.

We must take three psychological and relational steps to begin to accomplish this. First, individuals and subgroups within the system must withdraw the images, feelings, ideas, and roles that they have projected onto one another. Perhaps education about psychological and social projection and objectification must precede conversations and studies about sexuality and sexual orientation.

Second, persons in various positions and levels of power must publicly acknowledge the institution's mixed messages with regard to sexuality and sexual orientation and the resulting psychological impact of the double bind in which lesbian/gay/bisexual persons live. This affirmation of the interplay of theological and psychological factors and empathetic understanding of the tensions with which lesbian/gay/bisexual persons live can foster a feeling of safety, enabling persons to speak of their true selves within communal relationships, trusting that they will be heard.

Finally, throughout the system, safe places and networks must be created for lesbian, gay, bisexual, and heterosexual persons who risk their position and power within the institution by challenging its heterosexism and homophobia. These places and networks must embody the call to the church as the liberating community and must bring people through the wilderness. These need to be worshiping communities, whose liturgy is born out of its praxis of justice-seeking. Practically, these subcommunities need to provide economic and social support and safety, as well as psychological and spiritual community. For example, Spirit of the Mountains is trying to establish a fund to help gay and lesbian parents fight for custody and/or visitation if they have been denied access to their children on the basis of sexual orientation.

For far too long, openly gay/lesbian/bisexual persons have been denied opportunities for leadership and participation in the United Church of Christ. Many gay/lesbian/bisexual clergy know that to come out often means unemployment in the church (and always means a very long search process), no matter how affirmed our gifts for ministry have been. This must change. If we were good pastors when closeted, then we are better pastors when liberated. Energy that we once spent denying our identity and silently internalizing attitudes of shame, low self-esteem, and fear now can be freed up for more appropriate and significant tasks of ministry. In addition, the experience of being embraced by the community of faith for who we really are, as children of God, can do nothing less than radically empower our vision and action as leaders in the body of Christ. At present, the church is rejecting a profound source of creative and powerful leadership.

Openly lesbian/gay/bisexual persons must be placed in positions of authority and leadership. We need "out" teachers, pastors, moderators, deacons, conference ministers, denominational executives, etc. Lesbian/gay/bisexual persons cannot accomplish these ends alone. Search committees and those already in positions of authority and influence must actively seek those who have been left out, while providing some sense of safety and support for lesbian/gay bisexual persons willing to risk the homophobic fallout that inevitably occurs.

As has been related repeatedly through the ONA study process, churches must break the shroud of silence that has been covering them for generations. Not to actively express hostility to gay/lesbian/bisexual persons is not enough. Churches must actively express support and advocacy for gay/lesbian/bisexual persons. There are numerous ways this can and must be done.

Churches can engage in the ONA study process and publicly proclaim their welcoming of gay/lesbian/bisexual persons. To vote an ONA resolution is not enough. If the people you are welcoming have been brutally beaten (figuratively and literally) for generations with Christian rhetoric, then you must *work* to welcome them. Advertise in gay/lesbian/bisexual newspapers. Offer a public service of healing and reconciliation. Provide meeting space for gay, lesbian, and bisexual groups. State what ONA means on your church sign. Think creatively about the numerous ways to extend hospitality to persons who have been badly hurt.

Pastors can include examples of gay/lesbian/bisexual persons in sermons, prayers, and liturgical imagery. Worship services can include coming-out rites and rituals. The need to seek forgiveness from homophobia and heterosexism can be lifted up during pastoral prayers. Deacons can make certain that milestones of all kinds of family units are celebrated in church life (for example, gay and lesbian anniversaries and unions honored in the same way as heterosexual marriages). Church members can educate themselves about the concerns of gay/lesbian/bisexual persons. Heterosexual people can read books and magazines and attend events in order to learn more about what is like to be gay, lesbian, or bisexual. Everyone can become involved, individually and communally, in the work for civil and human rights for lesbian/gay/bisexual persons. Attend the area pride march with a church banner. Get involved opposing anti-gay legislation. Become active in the political efforts to secure basic civil rights. *Never* let a homophobic joke or statement go unchallenged. In other words, anything that churches do for heterosexual persons and/or persons victimized by oppression and violence, they can do publicly and clearly for gay/lesbian/bisexual persons. This is the only way that silence can and will be broken.

As has been said throughout this book, this will not be possible without first acknowledging the psychological, systemic, and theological functions that homophobia and heterosexism serve, and then risking the withdrawing of projections and objectifications. One cannot expect this to happen at all levels of the institution at once. Therefore, the interfacing of various subsystems and suprasystems is necessary for positive change to take place. Communication, feedback loops, and communication structures are critical in the work for change.

Until the church and society become truly open and affirming, in all times and places, lesbian/gay/bisexual persons will continue to have many unique concerns. Being gay/lesbian/bisexual and being surrounded by homophobia creates significant loss, fear, and suffering. The church needs to provide a community in which these concerns can be addressed. At this point, that seems to be happening in two primary ways. First, we must incorporate the concerns of lesbian/gay/bisexual persons into the mainstream of church life. The ways in which we can accomplish this are listed above. Second, we must support lesbian/gay/bisexual persons in addressing *our own needs* in unique environments. For example, an established congregation can provide support for gay/lesbian/bisexual discussion and support groups. In other areas, new congregations with specific outreach to the lesbian/gay/bisexual community must emerge and be supported by the church at large. I know that Spirit of the Mountains would not be as successful as we are without the support of the First Congregational Church, UCC, where we gather.

Since the church is a system, it can not only tolerate, but greatly benefit, from a diversity of approaches in a number of different places and levels of church life. It is hoped that some day the local congregation's gay/lesbian/bisexual support group will be as "normal" as the women's social group or the men's prayer breakfast. Until that day comes, however, we have significant work to do. Gay/lesbian/bisexual people need to care for ourselves, and take ourselves and our needs for spirituality and community seriously. If there is not a Welcoming Congregation in your area, seek out or create some kind of gay/lesbian/bisexual community of faith.

My prayer is that someday the church will be fully open and affirming, empowering all to celebrate the diversity of sexuality and the ongoing creative and liberating love of God. I hope that lesbian, gay, bisexual, and heterosexual persons will affirm one another in true solidarity and community. I yearn for the day when lesbian/gay/bisexual persons and their chosen families will be married, buried, and celebrated in the church with the same affection and intimacy as heterosexual family units. I look to the time when sexual orientation is honestly not an issue in the ordination and call of clergy, and when there is openly gay/lesbian/bisexual lay leadership in all areas of church life.

We are being led together on a journey of healing that is often fraught with pain, fear, backlash, and injustice. Nonetheless, if we trust God's leading, whatever our sexual orientation, empowering one another to "come out" as our fullest selves, we will be able to "stay in" the body of Christ with integrity, love, and vision. This becomes the essence and manifestation of theological, spiritual, and psychological liberation. Then, and only then, will we make it through the wilderness.

Questions for Discussion

1. What is the most surprising or startling insight you gained about gay/lesbian/bisexual people as a result of reading this book?

2. What insights have you gained about gay/lesbian/bisexual people that empower you to create justice in the church and society?

3. How have you observed the religious right's intolerance toward gay/lesbian/bisexual persons and others, both locally and nationally?

4. If you are gay, lesbian, or bisexual, have you come out to your church? Why or why not? To whom do you need to speak, and what do you need to say to break the silence about your life?

5. If you are heterosexual, have you listened to gay/lesbian/bisexual persons tell their stories? How can you listen and learn more?

6. Has your congregation voted to become a Welcoming Congregation? If so, have you become actively involved in advocacy and justice-making with the gay/lesbian/bisexual community in your area? If not, why not? How can you advocate for gay/lesbian/bisexual persons at this time?

7. How might you include this justice commitment in your prayer and spiritual life? How might your church include it in its worship and liturgy?

8. What can you do, as an individual and as a congregation, to join the gay/lesbian/bisexual movement toward liberation?

Appendix A

Interview Questionnaire

1. Identifying data: age, gender, sexual orientation, clergy/laity status.
2. Were you raised as a child in a religion? Which one? Do you remember any references as a child to homosexuality in the church?
3. How do you identify yourself religiously? (e.g., Christian, Jewish, agnostic, creation-centered, atheist, post-Christian, feminist Christian, etc.)
4. Do you participate now in any kind of religious community? Where and what is your level of participation?
5. Have you experienced homophobia/heterosexism in the church?
6. If so, please describe one or two of the most painful experiences, images, or moments of homophobia/heterosexism you have had in the church.
7. Have you experienced any moments, events, images of healing in regard to homophobia/heterosexism in the church? If so, please describe.
8. If you could say anything to "the church" in regard to homophobia/heterosexism, what would you say?

Appendix B

Welcoming Congregation Statements
from Several Denominations;
UCC Pronouncements and Resolutions
regarding Lesbian/Gay/Bisexual Concerns

Spirit of the Mountains, Concord, New Hampshire: Mission Statement

The following is read in unison at the beginning of every celebration of worship.

Spirit of the Mountains is a community of gay and straight people that answers God's call to bring peace, justice, dignity and affirmation to all people through worship, pastoral care and support, education, social action and service.

Resolution of the Members and Friends of Spirit of the Mountains (Passed by Consensus, May 23, 1993)

As an open and affirming lesbian/gay/bisexual/straight community for peace and justice, we resolve to covenant with each other, with God's help,

To live actively the Christian principle to love our neighbors as ourselves;

To affirm our dedication to prayer, study and understanding of issues of peace and justice in ourselves, our relationships, our families, our community, our state, and our world;

To speak and to act to resolve words and deeds of injustice and violence in ourselves, our relationships, our families, our community, our state, our world—whenever and wherever our prayer, study, and understanding lead us;

To speak and act in the knowledge that silence in the presence of unjust acts is unacceptable;

To remember the vision and promise God that the lion and lamb shall lie down together.

Knowing that a vision of an open and affirming, just and peaceful world begins with the work of God through each of us, we further resolve in a spirit of love and hope,

To let it be known to all people of good will that we are dedicated to provide a safe place for people to converse with God and each other, regardless of creed, color, religion, gender, age, mental or physical health, disability, national origin, cultural background, economic status, or sexual orientation;

To find and use effective, peaceful, creative ways, in thought and word, to settle conflicts;

To maintain a spirit of responsiveness and caring towards all of God's Creation: all people, all creatures, and the planet on which we live;

To work together with others, to build a world of peace, openness, kindness, responsibility, affirmation, and justice,

In the name of the all-loving Creator.

Zion United Church of Christ, Henderson, Kentucky: An Open and Affirming Congregation

The people of Zion United Church of Christ in Henderson, Kentucky, on this twenty-second day of May 1994, do declare ourselves to be an "Open and Affirming Congregation" within the United Church of Christ. As an Open and Affirming Congregation:

We believe that the Gospel of Jesus Christ calls the church to be open to all people, which includes those among us who are gay, lesbian, or bisexual.

We recognize that gay men, lesbians, and bisexuals have been instrumental within the church throughout its history.

We confess that the church has too often and for too long been the major instrument of oppression for gay, lesbian, and bisexual people, by perpetuating discriminatory practices against clergy, laity, and staff, and by denying the full humanity of those with differing sexual orientations.

We accept God's call to love our neighbors as we love ourselves without being judgmental (Matt. 7:1–2) nor disparaging of others (Luke 18:9–14). In light of evolving biblical, theological, medical, biological, and psychological understandings, we realize the need for the church to become Open and Affirming.

We celebrate the rich diversity within Zion United Church of Christ and rejoice in the many talents and gifts that all have to offer.

We acknowledge that the church has remained conspicuously silent with regard to its ministry with persons living with HIV/AIDS. We welcome and support all persons affected, including and not limited to the gay, lesbian, and bisexual community.

We affirm that the struggle against homophobia and heterosexism is an ongoing process, which requires both an individual and communal commitment to prayer, study, and action. We commit ourselves to continual evaluation and to the support and love of one another in this difficult and joyful pilgrimage.

May God bless and empower us in our journey toward faithfulness.

Park Avenue Christian Church, New York City: Open and Affirming Statement

We affirm Christ's call to love God with all that we are and our neighbor as ourselves. Therefore, we pledge ourselves to be open to and affirming of all people regardless of gender, race, age, culture, ethnic background, sexual orientation, economic circumstance, family configuration, or difference in ability. All who affirm the love of Christ in their lives are welcome into this community and to share fully in its life and ministry. In response to the grace which Christ has given to us, we glorify God, we commit ourselves to growth in the Spirit, and we rejoice in the worth, gifts and dignity of every person as a child of God. Amen.

(Recommended to the Official Board by the Board of Elders April 5, 1992. Adopted without dissent at the May 17, 1992 meeting of the Official Board.)

The First Presbyterian and Trinity Church, South Orange, New Jersey

As a community of faith, the congregation of The First Presbyterian and Trinity Church of South Orange, New Jersey, welcomes all who believe in Jesus Christ and acknowledge Him Lord and Savior, denying no one full participation in its life and leadership on the basis of race, ethnic origin, worldly condition, age, sex, sexual orientation, or any other particular element of his or her total humanity. We believe that the errors of society which have resulted in oppression and despair are not the ways of God, and we seek not to assume judgment upon our sisters and brothers in our journey of faith. Instead we seek more light on the ways in which we can offer our support and our love to all the children of God.

In accordance with this total view, we join with "More Light" churches and others seeking fairness, openness, honesty, and the affirmation of all who declare their membership in the body of Christ.

Grant Park-Aldersgate United Methodist Church, Atlanta, Georgia: A Statement of Reconciliation

God has created all people, finding all that God made to be good. Divine love and grace are offered to everyone, without any reservation. The community of God's people, the church, is called to be holy and to be a priesthood, inviting others to be in the covenant relationship with God. The church is to be a reconciling body; to offer reconciliation between God and humankind, and between persons with each other.

We of the Grant Park-Aldersgate United Methodist Church strive to be God's witnesses to all persons, regardless of race, gender, age, national origin, or sexual orientation. We affirm lesbian women and gay men as full participants in our congregation. We will advocate their rights as human beings and as Christians.

We recognize that gay men and lesbian women are discriminated against in our society. We regret the actions of those who fear these brothers and sisters. We believe that God has made all persons of equal worth, and all God's children are to be respected and cherished.

We believe that we have been reconciled to God through Jesus Christ, and we intend to be a reconciling congregation. We invite others to join with us in our efforts to work for a just and caring society.

United Church of Christ: Resolution Affirming Gay, Lesbian and Bisexual Persons and Their Ministries (Adopted by the Eighteenth General Synod, Norfolk, Virginia, July 2, 1991)

WHEREAS, in the words of the apostle Paul, we know that "the whole creation has been groaning in travail" and we, too, feel these pains as we struggle to grow in our understanding of human sexuality; and

WHEREAS, the actions of General Synods 10, 11, 14, 15, 16, and 17 have supported human rights of all persons in church and society, regardless of sexual orientation; and

WHEREAS, lesbian, gay, bisexual persons, and their families have shared their gifts for ministry throughout the church, and through their stories and ministries the United Church of Christ has come to a deeper understanding of the diversity of God's creation and the inclusiveness of God's call;

THEREFORE, BE IT RESOLVED, that the Eighteenth General Synod boldly affirms, celebrates, and embraces the gifts for ministry of lesbian, gay, and bisexual persons, and faithfully continues to work for justice in our church and society.

BE IT FURTHER RESOLVED, that the Eighteenth General Synod calls upon local churches, associations, and conferences to adopt an Open and Affirming policy. (i.e., a nondiscrimination policy and a covenant of openness and affirmation of persons of lesbian, gay and bisexual orientation within the community of faith (cf.: General Synod 15).

BE IT FURTHER RESOLVED, the Eighteenth General Synod urgently calls upon local churches, associations, and conferences to engage in a disciplined dialogue in which the biblical and theological foundations for congregations to be Open and Affirming of gay, lesbian, and bisexual persons are prayerfully discussed in light of the teachings of Jesus Christ and our Christian vocation to live as communities of grace and reconciliation. The instrumentalities are requested to provide study resources for the United Church of Christ.

BE IT FURTHER RESOLVED, the Eighteenth General Synod calls upon local churches, associations, and conferences to extend their welcome and support to openly lesbian, gay, and bisexual students in care, and to facilitate the ordination and placement of qualified lesbian, gay, and bisexual candidates.

FINALLY, the Eighteenth General Synod invites all persons of the United Church of Christ to experience the struggle and joy of the journey towards Openness and Affirmation of all lesbian, gay, and bisexual persons as children of God in the community of faith.

United Church of Christ: Call for Congregations to Declare Themselves Open and Affirming (Adopted by the Fifteenth General Synod, Ames, Iowa, June 2, 1985)

WHEREAS, the apostle Paul said that, as Christians, we are many members, but we are one body in Christ (Rom. 12:4), and Jesus calls us to love our neighbors as ourselves (Mark 12:31) without being judgmental (Matt. 7:1–2) nor disparaging of others (Luke 18:9–14); and

WHEREAS, recognizing that many persons of lesbian, gay, and bisexual orientation are already members of the church through baptism and confirmation and that these people have talents and gifts to offer the United Church of Christ, and that the UCC has historically affirmed a rich diversity in its theological and biblical perspectives; and

WHEREAS, the Tenth through Fourteenth General Synods have adopted resolutions encouraging the inclusion, and affirming the human rights, of lesbian, gay and bisexual people within the UCC; and

WHEREAS, the Executive Council of the United Church of Christ adopted in 1980 "a program of Equal Employment Opportunity which does not discriminate against any employee or applicant because of . . . sexual orientation"; and

WHEREAS, many parts of the church have remained conspicuously silent despite the continuing injustice of institutionalized discrimination, instances of senseless violence and setbacks in civil rights protection by the Supreme Court; and

WHEREAS, the church has often perpetuated discriminatory practices and has been unwilling to affirm the full humanness of clergy, laity, and staff with lesbian, gay, and bisexual orientation, who experience isolation, ostracism, and fear of (or actual) loss of employment; and

WHEREAS, we are called by Christ's example to proclaim release to the captives and set at liberty the oppressed (Luke 4:18); and

WHEREAS, examples of covenant of Openness and Affirmation and Nondiscrimination Policy may be found in the following examples.

Example 1: Covenant of Openness and Affirmation

We know, with Paul, that as Christians, we are many members, but are one body in Christ—members of one another, and that we all have different gifts. With Jesus, we affirm that we are called to love our neighbors as ourselves, that we are called to act as agents of reconciliation and wholeness within the world and within the church itself.

We know that lesbian, gay, and bisexual people are often scorned by the church, and devalued and discriminated against both in the church and in society. We commit ourselves to caring and concern for lesbian, gay and bisexual sisters and brothers by affirming that:

- *we believe that lesbian, gay, and bisexual people share with all others the worth that comes from being unique individuals;*

- *we welcome lesbian, gay, and bisexual people to join our congregation in the same spirit and manner used in the acceptance of any new members;*

- *we recognize the presence of ignorance, fear, and hatred in the church and in our culture, and covenant to not discriminate on the basis of sexual orientation, or any other irrelevant factor, and we seek to include and support those who, because of this fear and prejudice, find themselves in exile from a spiritual community;*

- *we seek to address the needs and advocate the concerns of lesbian, gay, and bisexual people in our church and in society by actively encouraging church instrumentalities and secular governmental bodies to adopt and implement policies of nondiscrimination; and,*

- *we join together as a covenantal community, to celebrate and share our common communion and the reassurance that we are indeed created by God, reconciled by Christ, and empowered by the grace of the Holy Spirit.*

Example 2: Inclusive Nondiscrimination Policy

We do not discriminate against any person, group or organization in hiring, promotion, membership, appointment, use of facility, provision of services, or funding on the basis of race, gender, age, sexual orientation, faith, nationality, ethnicity, marital status, or physical disability.

THEREFORE, the Fifteenth General Synod of the United Church of Christ encourages a policy of nondiscrimination in employment, volunteer service, and membership policies with regard to sexual orientation; encourages associations, Conferences, and all related organizations to adopt a similar policy; and encourages the congregations of the United Church of

Christ to adopt a nondiscrimination policy and a Covenant of Openness and Affirmation of persons of lesbian, gay, and bisexual orientation within the community of faith.

United Church of Christ: Resolution on Homosexuals and the Law (Adopted by the Council for Christian Social Action, April 12, 1969)

Preface

Christian love for God and our neighbor in God impels us to cherish the life and liberty of all [persons]. Even while we proclaim a unity under God which transcends our division, and while we find in Christ our measure for being human, we still honor variations among [persons] in their political loyalties, lifestyles, and sexual preferences. Love is meaningless which does not cherish in others the freedom to be different from ourselves. Faith in the sovereign God is likewise betrayed when it does not accord to [God] rather than ourselves the ultimate judgment of the moral limits of human variation. This is our Christian warrant for championing the fullest civil as well as religious liberties.

In no other dimension of life is such liberality more difficult or more important that in attitudes towards sex. The weight of Christian tradition, while commending chastity as a vocation, has clearly stressed faithfully monogamous, heterosexual marriage as the normal context for personal growth, sexual fulfillment, procreation, and the rearing of children. Sexual intimacy in any other context still tends to be viewed by the church as a substitute for marriage or a lapse from it, but as reprehensible in any case.

Such a Christian ideal, worthy as it is, should not blind us to variations and limitations which may preclude that ideal for many. Nor should it lead Christians to a rigid and graceless moralism which proscribes and persecutes those unable by constitution or circumstance to fulfill their Christian hope. We believe that the church, which has long honored both chastity and marriage as vocations, must also learn to cherish, and not merely to condemn, those whose sexual need and loneliness may prove importunate—though unmarried, unmarriageable, widowed, or homosexual.

Among these conditions, homosexuality has proved by far the most difficult for most of us to accept and to accord respect and freedom either in the church or in public life. Fortunately, new insight is available. For example, modern Bible scholarship suggests that, while homosexuality is condemned in the Old and New Testaments, its seriousness has been exaggerated by wrenching scriptural verses out of context. As elsewhere, (e.g., Eph. 6:5: "Slaves be obedient to those who are your earthly masters"), censorious and self-righteous selection and use of Scripture has further obscured the truth as well as betraying canons of Christian charity.

Again, while even medical specialists are divided on the nature and the irreversibility of homosexuality, its causes are now better understood, its extent more accurately assessed, and cruel cultural myths alleging danger to society from homosexual persons have been dispelled. We also now understand that sexual differences in personality and preference constitute a continuum of variation rather than an absolute polarity.

According to the most conservative estimates, at least one out of every twenty men and women are predominately homosexual in orientation. The United States, Germany, and Austria remain the only countries in the Western world still proscribing homosexual practices as a criminal violation. In our nation known homosexuals are excluded from civil as well as military service, widely denied jobs and residence, and socially ostracized. Those not known are forced into a clandestine double life of dishonesty and subterfuge, with constant risk of blackmail, unemployment, and criminal prosecution as well, in all states except Illinois.

The Council for Christian Social Action believes that the time is long overdue for our churches to be enlisted in the cause of justice and compassion for homosexual persons as well as for other socially rejected minorities. Clearly there are profound pastoral responsibilities unmet by most churches for homosexual persons in their own midst. Yet our particular concern as a council is for the legal establishment of civil liberties—for whose denial we in the churches bear substantial blame.

The members of our council commend traditional Christian ideals of sex, marriage, and family life. Yet we believe that legal prohibition of sexual behavior should be limited to protecting men and women from sexual coercion, children from sexual exploitation, and society from offensive public display of sexual behavior.

In light of these considerations, we have adopted the following resolution:

Resolution

WHEREAS homosexual practices between consenting adults in private endanger none of the properly protective functions of civil law; and

WHEREAS laws against consensual homosexual practices between adults in private violate the right of privacy and are virtually unenforceable, except through the abhorrent practices of police entrapment and enticement; and

WHEREAS such laws have no effect on the degree of homosexuality (as indicated by various studies abroad showing that homosexuality exists to no greater extent in countries without such laws than in the United States); and

WHEREAS present laws and government practices regarding employment and military service of homosexuals are based on false assumptions about the nature of homosexuality in general and the danger of homosexuals to society in particular;

THEREFORE, the Council for Christian Social Action (CCSA) hereby declares its opposition to all laws which make private homosexual relations between consenting adults a crime and thus urges their repeal.

FURTHER, the CCSA expresses its opposition to the total exclusion of homosexuals from public employment and from enlistment and induction into the armed forces, especially the dismissal of less-than-honorable discharges from the armed forces for homosexual practices with consenting adults in private. The CCSA supports dismissal of homosexuals from public employment and from the armed forces and their prosecution under the law when they have been found guilty of homosexual practices in public, against children or minors, or where force is used.

FURTHER, the CCSA opposes, where they exist, police practices of entrapment and enticement in their attempts to enforce laws against homosexual practices and solicitation.

FURTHER, the CCSA encourages the United Church of Christ conferences, associations, and local churches to hold seminars, consultations, conferences, etc., for honest and open discussion of the nature of homosexuality in our society.

Appendix C

Christian Organizations Focusing on Lesbian and Gay Concerns in the United States

The following resource list is based primarily on a compilation by Martin Rock:

Advance
c/o Thomas Hirsch
4001–C Maple Avenue
Dallas TX 75219

Affirmation/Mormons
P.O. Box 46022
Los Angeles CA 90046

Affirmation/United Methodists
P.O. Box 1021
Evanston IL 60204

American Baptists Concerned
872 Erie Street
Oakland CA 94610

Axios—Eastern and Orthodox Christian Gay Men
and Women
328 W. 17th Street, Apt. 4F
New York NY 10011

Brethren/Mennonite Council for Lesbian and Gay
Concerns
P.O. Box 65724
Washington DC 20035–5724

CLOUT: Christian Lesbians Out Together
c/o Selisse Berry
P.O. Box 460808
San Francisco CA 94146–0808

Common Bond (former Jehovah's Witnesses and
   Mormons)
P.O. Box 405
Ellwood PA 16117

Conference for Catholic Lesbians
P.O. Box 436 Planetarium Station
New York NY 10024

Dignity, Inc. (Roman Catholics)
1500 Massachusetts Avenue, N.W., Suite 11
Washington DC 20005

Emergence International (Christian Scientists)
P.O. Box 9161
San Rafael CA 94912–9161

Evangelicals Concerned
c/o Dr. Ralph Blair
311 E. 72nd Street, Suite 1–G
New York NY 10021

Friends for Lesbian/Gay Concerns (Quakers)
P.O. Box 222
Sumneytown PA 18084

Gay, Lesbian, and Affirming Disciples Alliance
(Christian Church, Disciples of Christ)
P.O. Box 19223
Indianapolis IN 46219–0223

Holiness Alliance for Gay/Lesbian Ministries
P.O. Box 60098
Nashville TN 37206–0098

Honesty (Southern Baptist Convention)
c/o David Tribble
603 Quail's Run Road, Apt. C-1
Louisville KY 40207

Integrity, Inc. (Episcopalians)
P.O. Box 19561
Washington DC 20036–0561

Lifeline Baptists (all Baptists)
c/o Rev. James T. Williams Sr., MD
8150 Lakecrest Drive
Greenbelt MD 20770

Lutherans Concerned
P.O. Box 10461
Fort Dearborn Station
Chicago IL 60610–0461

National Gay Pentecostal Alliance
P.O. Box 1391
Schenectady NY 12301–1391

Other Sheep: Multicultural Ministries with Sexual
    Minorities
Dr. Thomas Hanks, Executive Director
Lavalle 376–2D
1047 Buenos Aires, Argentina
U.S. Address:
319 N. 4th Street, Suite 902
St. Louis MO 63102

Presbyterians for Lesbian and Gay Concerns
P.O. Box 38
New Brunswick NJ 08903–0038

Reach Out (former Jehovah's Witnesses and Mormons)
P.O. Box 1173
Clackamas OR 97015

Reconciling Congregation Program (United Methodists)
3801 N. Keeler Avenue
Chicago IL 60641–3007

Reformed Church in American Gay Caucus
P.O. Box 8174
Philadelphia PA 19101–8174

SDA Kinship International (Seventh Day Adventists)
P.O. Box 3840
Los Angeles CA 90078–3840

T-E-N (The Evangelical Network)
c/o Fred L. Pattison
P.O. Box 32441
Phoenix AZ 85064

Unitarian Universalists for Lesbian and Gay Concerns
25 Beacon Street
Boston MA 02108

United Church Coalition for Lesbian/Gay Concerns (UCC)
18 N. College Street
Athens OH 45701

Unity Fellowship Church
5149 W. Jefferson Boulevard
Los Angeles CA 90016

Universal Fellowship of Metropolitan Community
    Churches
500 Santa Monica Boulevard, Suite 304
Los Angeles CA 90029

Programs in the Welcoming Movement

For more information about the program in your denomination, please contact:

American Baptist
Welcoming and Affirming Baptists
P.O. Box 2596
Attleboro Falls MA 02763

Brethren/Mennonite
Supportive Congregations
P.O. Box 6300
Minneapolis MN 55406

Disciples of Christ
Allen Harris, Open and Affirming (O&A)
1010 Park Avenue
New York NY 10028
(212) 288–3246

Lutheran (ELCA)
Judy Bond, Reconciled in Christ
1722 Hollinwood Drive
Alexandria VA 22307
(703) 768–4915

Methodist
James Preston, Reconciling Congregations
3801 N. Keeler Avenue
Chicago IL 60641
(312) 736–5526

Presbyterian
William Capel, More Light Churches
123R W. Church Street
Champaign IL 61820
(217) 355–9825

Unitarian Universalist
Meg Riley, Welcoming Congregations
P.O. Box 11201
Takoma Park MD 20913
(202) 726–2195

United Church of Christ
Ann B. Day, Open and Affirming (ONA)
P.O. Box 403
Holden MA 01520–0403
(508) 856–9316

Notes

Introduction: The Significance of Coming Out While Staying In—A Personal Journey of Spirituality and Sexuality

1. "Lead Me, Lord," *Pilgrim Hymnal* (Boston: The Pilgrim Press, 1958), no. 524.

2. Tom Conry, *We Shall Not Be Silent* (Portland, Oreg.: OCP Publications, 1995).

3. Salvador Minuchin, *Families and Family Therapy* (Cambridge: Harvard University Press, 1974).

4. James B. Nelson, *Embodiment: An Approach to Sexuality and Christian Theology* (Minneapolis: Augsburg Press, 1978), 198–99.

5. John Boswell, *Christianity, Social Tolerance, and Homosexuality: Gay People in Western Europe from the Beginning of the Christian Era to the Fourteenth Century* (Chicago: University of Chicago Press, 1980), 135.

6. George Weinberg, *Society and the Healthy Homosexual* (New York: St. Martin's Press, 1972), 1.

7. Warren Blumenfeld and Diane Raymond, *Looking at Gay and Lesbian Life* (Boston: Beacon Press, 1989), 244.

1. Family Secrets: Gay/Lesbian/Bisexuality; Homophobia and Heterosexism in the Church

1. Blumenfeld and Raymond, *Looking at Gay and Lesbian Life*.

2. Jonathan Katz, *Gay American History: Lesbians and Gay Men in the U.S.A.* (New York: Meridian Books, 1992).

3. Linda D. Garnets and Douglas C. Kimmel., eds. *Psychological Perspectives on Lesbian and Gay Male Experiences* (New York: Columbia University Press, 1993).

4. Irvashi Vaid, *Virtual Equality: The Mainstreaming of Gay and Lesbian Liberation* (New York: Anchor Books, 1995), 57.

5. Committee on Gay and Lesbian Concerns, "Avoiding Heterosexual Bias in Language," *American Psychologist* 46, no. 9 (Sept. 1991): 973–74.

6. Sari H. Dworkin, "The Role of Bisexuality in Lesbian and Gay Psychology," paper presented at the national convention of the American Psychological Association, New York City, 11 August 1995, pp. 3–4. Reprints available from Sari Dworkin, Ph.D., California State University, Department of Counseling and Special Education, 5005 N. Maple, Fresno, CA 93740–0003.

7. Vaid, *Virtual Equality*, 8.

8. For more information, contact Parents and Friends of Lesbians and Gays, 1101 14th Street, N.W., Suite 1030, Washington, DC 20005, or the National Gay and Lesbian Task Force, 2320 17th Street, N.W., Washington, DC 20009.

9. Blumenfeld and Raymond, *Looking at Gay and Lesbian Life*, 226.

10. Ibid., 226–30.

11. Suzanne Pharr, *Homophobia: A Weapon of Sexism* (Little Rock: Chardon Press, 1988), 53–64.

12. Vaid, *Virtual Equality*, 3.

13. George Weinberg, *Society and the Healthy Homosexual*, 1.

14. Ibid., 4.

15. Ibid., 1–20.

16. Ibid., 8–20.

17. Murray Bowen, *Family Therapy in Clinical Practice* (Northvale, N.J.: Jason Arons, 1985), 322.

18. Blumenfeld and Raymond, *Looking at Gay and Lesbian Life*, 244–45.

19. Carter Heyward, "Coming Out and Relational Empowerment: A Lesbian Feminist Theological Perspective," Stone Center Colloquium Series, Episcopal Divinity School, Cambridge, Mass. (1989), no. 4, 191–92.

20. Blumenfeld and Raymond, *Looking at Gay and Lesbian Life*, 259–62.

21. Christopher Carrington, "The Respectable Gay Men and Lesbians: A Negotiated-Order Approach to the Inclusion of Gay Men and Lesbians in the Congregational Life of Liberal Protestantism," Ph.D. diss., University of Massachusetts, Dept. of Sociology, 1993, 33–35.

22. Liz Margolies, Martha Becker, and Karla Jackson-Brewer, "Internalized Homophobia: Identifying and Treating the Oppressor Within," in *Lesbian Psychologies: Explorations and Challenges,* ed. Boston Lesbian Psychologies Collective (Urbana and Chicago: University of Illinois Press, 1987), 230.

23. Ibid., 231–33.

24. Nancy Gartrell, "Issues in Psychotherapy with Lesbian Women," Stone Center Paper, Stone Center for Developmental Services, Wellesley College, Wellesley, Mass., 1984, 1.

25. Ibid., 8.

26. Heyward, "Coming Out and Relational Empowerment," 5.

27. Blumenfeld and Raymond, *Looking at Gay and Lesbian Life,* 234.

28. Boswell, *Christianity, Social Tolerance, and Homosexuality,* 6.

29. Ibid., 15.

30. Mel White, *Stranger at the Gate: To Be Gay and Christian in America* (New York: Penguin Books, 1994), 224–25.

2. Where We Are, Where We Have Been, and Where We Are Going: A Brief Overview of the Gay/Lesbian/Bisexual Movement in Mainline Churches

1. "Growing in Faith: The Lesbian/Gay Christian Movement," *Open Hands: Reconciling Ministries with Lesbians and Gay Men* 5, no. 3 (winter 1990). Published by United Methodists for Lesbian/Gay Concerns.

2. Reconciling Congregation Program, "Welcoming Churches: A Growing Ecumenical Movement," *Open Hands: Resources of Ministries Affirming the Diversity of Human Sexuality* 8, no. 3 (winter 1993).

3. James D. Anderson, "The Lesbian and Gay Liberation Movement in the Churches of the United States, 1969–1993, with Special Reference to Presbyterians for Lesbian and Gay Concerns, 1974–1993." Rutgers University and Presbyterians for Lesbian and Gay Concerns. A revised version, titled "The Lesbian and Gay Liberation Movement in the Presbyterian Church, U.S.A., 1974–1995," will appear in the *Journal of Homosexuality,* ed. John P. DeCecco, published by Haworth Press, 10 Alice Street, Binghamton, NY 13904–1580.

4. Boswell, *Christianity, Social Tolerance, and Homosexuality.*

5. John Boswell, *Same-Sex Unions in Premodern Europe* (New York: Vintage Press, 1995).

3. The Body of Christ: Functional or Dysfunctional System?

1. Minuchin, *Families and Family Therapy,* 89.

2. Ibid., 89.

3. *The New Century Hymnal* (Cleveland: The Pilgrim Press, 1995), no. 316.

4. Earl Thompson, class lecture, Andover Newton Theological School, Andover, Mass., September 17, 1991.

5. Minuchin, *Families and Family Therapy,* 2.

6. Vaid, *Virtual Equality,* 1.

7. Earl Thompson, class lecture, Andover Newton Theological School, Andover, Mass., September 17, 1991.

8. Minuchin, *Families and Family Therapy,* 4–5.

9. Claudia Black, *It Will Never Happen to Me: Children of Alcoholics* (New York: Ballantine Press, 1981), 24.

10. Ibid., 31.

11. Cited in Michael Nichols, *Family Therapy: Concepts and Methods* (Boston: Allyn & Bacon, 1984), 269–70.

12. Ibid., 584.

13. Minuchin, *Families and Family Therapy,* 110.

14. Ibid., 119.

15. Deborah Anna Luepnitz, *The Family Interpreted: Feminist Theory in Clinical Practice* (New York: Basic Books, 1988), 65.

16. Murray Bowen, *Family Therapy in Clinical Practice,* 205.

17. Ibid., 200.

18. Pharr, *Homophobia,* 8.

19. Sheldon Cashdan, *Object Relations Therapy—Using the Relationship* (New York: W. W. Norton, 1988), 34.

20. White, *Stranger at the Gate,* 338–39.

21. Cashdan, *Object Relations Therapy,* 55–56.

22. Suzanna Rose, "Sexual Pride and Shame in Lesbians," in *Lesbian and Gay Psychology: Theory, Practice, and Clinical Applications,* ed. Beverly Greene and Gregory M. Herek (Thousand Oaks, Calif.: Sage Publications, 1994), 72.

23. Cashdan, *Object Relations Therapy,* 45.

24. Quoted by Earl Thompson, class lecture, Andover Newton Theological School, Andover, Mass., September 17, 1991.

4. A Liberating Theology of the Church

1. Nelson, *Embodiment,* 259.

2. Gary David Comstock, *Gay Theology without Apology* (Cleveland: The Pilgrim Press, 1992), 19.

3. Paul D. Hanson, *The People Called: The Growth of Community in the Bible* (San Francisco: Harper & Row, 1986), 467.

4. Cited in Comstock, *Gay Theology without Apology,* 109.

5. Reinhold Niebuhr, *Leaves from the Notebook of a Tamed Cynic* (Chicago: Willet, Clark, & Colby, 1929), 69.

6. George W. Webber, *Today's Church: A Community of Exiles and Pilgrims* (Nashville: Abingdon Press, 1979), 12.

7. Comstock, *Gay Theology without Apology,* 10.

8. Nelson, *Embodiment,* 259.

9. Presbyterian Church USA, General Assembly Special Committee on Human Sexuality, "Keeping Body and Soul Together: Sexuality, Spirituality, and Social Justice," *Reports to the 203rd General Assembly* (1991): 48.

10. Webber, *Today's Church,* 19.

5. The Journey toward Sexual and Spiritual Liberation

1. Gustavo Gutiérrez, *A Theology of Liberation* (Maryknoll, N.Y.: Orbis Press, 1973), 6.

2. Ibid., 13.

3. Ibid., 15.

4. Heyward, "Coming Out and Relational Empowerment," 11.

5. Susan Brooks Thistlethwaite and Mary Potter Engel, eds., *Lift Every Voice: Constructing Christian Theologies for the Underside* (San Francisco: HarperSanFrancisco, 1990), 7–8.

6. Ibid., 20.

7. Carter Heyward, *Speaking of Christ: A Lesbian Feminist Perspective* (New York: The Pilgrim Press, 1989), 26.

8. Ibid., 27.

9. Ibid., 28.

10. Ibid., 29.

11. Ibid., 28.

12. Ibid., 31.

13. Ibid., 31

6. Stories of Hurting, Stories of Healing: Lesbian, Gay, and Bisexual Persons Speak of Their Experiences in the Church

1. Carrington, "The Respectable Gay Men and Lesbians," 1.

2. Ibid., 45–46.

3. Nelle Morton, *The Journey Is Home* (Boston: Beacon Press, 1985).

4. Comstock, *Gay Theology without Apology*, 102.

5. Susan E. Davies and Eleanor H. Haney, *Redefining Sexual Ethics: A Sourcebook of Essays, Stories, and Poems* (Cleveland: The Pilgrim Press, 1991), 83.

6. This is taken from a 1993 Christmas letter sent to me by my friends, Peter Illgenfritz and Dave Schull, who after a long and faithful search have been called as co-associate pastors of the University Christian Church in Seattle, Washington, where their ministry is thriving.

7. Ibid.

7. *Conclusions, Implications, and Suggestions for Ministry*

1. Vaid, *Virtual Equality*, 307.

2. This button and quotation have become symbols for many gay/lesbian/bisexual activists in the church. They are found wherever gay/lesbian/bisexual people and our supporters gather.

3. Vaid, *Virtual Equality*, 310.

4. United Church Coalition for Lesbian/Gay Concerns, "Open and Affirming Churches in the UCC: Update '93, a Report from Sixty-Four ONA Congregations about Studying, Declaring, and Living an Open and Affirming Commitment," 1993, 17.

5. Ibid., 25.

Bibliography

Affirmation: United Methodists for Lesbian/Gay Concerns. "Growing in Faith: the Lesbian/Gay Christian Movement." *Open Hands: Reconciling Ministries with Lesbians and Gay Men 5*, no. 3 (winter 1990).

Anderson, James D. "The Lesbian and Gay Liberation Movement in the Churches of the United States, 1969–1993, with Special Reference to Presbyterians for Lesbian and Gay concerns, 1974–1993." Rutgers University and Presbyterians for Lesbian and Gay Concerns. A revised version, titled "The Lesbian and Gay Liberation Movement in the Presbyterian Church, U.S.A., 1974–1995," will appear in the *Journal of Homosexuality*, ed. John P. DeCecco, published by Haworth Press, 10 Alice Street, Binghamton, NY 13904–1580.

Batchelor, Edward, Jr., ed. *Homosexuality and Ethics*. New York: The Pilgrim Press, 1980.

Black, Claudia. *It Will Never Happen to Me: Children of Alcoholics*. New York: Ballantine Press, 1981.

Blumenfeld, Warren, and Diane Raymond. *Looking at Gay and Lesbian Life*. Boston: Beacon Press, 1989.

Boston Lesbian Psychologies Collective. *Lesbian Psychologies: Explorations and Challenges*. Urbana and Chicago: University of Illinois Press, 1987.

Boswell, John. *Christianity, Social Tolerance, and Homosexuality: Gay People in Western Europe from the Beginning of the Christian Era to the Fourteenth Century*. Chicago: University of Chicago Press, 1980.

———. *Same-Sex Unions in Premodern Europe*. New York: Vintage Press, 1995.

Bowen, Murray. *Family Therapy in Clinical Practice*. Northvale, N.J.: Jason Arons, 1985.

Carl, Douglas. *Counseling Same-Sex Couples*. New York: W. W. Norton, 1990.

Carrington, Christopher. "The Respectable Gay Men and Lesbians: A Negotiated-order Approach to the Inclusion of Gay Men and Lesbians in the Congregational Life of Liberal Protestantism." Ph.D. diss., University of Massachusetts, Dept. of Sociology, 1993.

Cashdan, Sheldon. *Object Relations Therapy—Using the Relationship*. New York: W. W. Norton, 1988.

Comstock, Gary David. *Gay Theology without Apology*. Cleveland: The Pilgrim Press, 1993.

Davies, Susan E., and Eleanor H. Haney, eds. *Redefining Sexual Ethics: A Sourcebook of Essays, Stories, and Poems.* Cleveland: The Pilgrim Press, 1991.

Dworkin, Sari H. "The Role of Bisexuality in Lesbian and Gay Psychology." Paper presented at the national convention of the American Psychological Association, New York City, 11 August 1995. Reprints available from Sari Dworkin, Ph.D., California State University, Department of Counseling and Special Education, 5005 N. Maple, Fresno, CA 93740–0003.

Friedman, Edwin. *Generation to Generation.* New York: Guilford Press, 1985.

Garnets, Linda D., and Douglas C. Kimmel, eds. *Psychological Perspectives on Lesbian and Gay Male Experiences.* New York: Columbia University Press, 1993.

Gartrell, Nancy. "Issues in Psychotherapy with Lesbian Women." Stone Center Paper, Stone Center for Developmental Services, Wellesley College, Wellesley, Mass., 1984.

Gerkin, Charles V., *The Living Human Document: Re-Visioning Pastoral Counseling in a Hermeneutical Mode.* Nashville: Abingdon Press, 1984.

Glaser, Chris. *Come Home! Reclaiming Spirituality and Community as Gay Men and Lesbians.* San Francisco: Harper & Row, 1990.

———. *Uncommon Calling: A Gay Man's Struggle to Serve the Church.* New York: Harper & Row, 1988.

———. *The Word Is Out: The Bible Reclaimed for Lesbians and Gay Men, 365 Daily Meditations.* San Francisco: HarperSanFrancisco, 1994.

Greene, Beverly, and Gregory M. Herek, eds. *Lesbian and Gay Psychology: Theory, Research, and Clinical Applications.* Thousand Oaks, Calif.: Sage Publications, 1994.

Gutiérrez, Gustavo. *A Theology of Liberation.* Maryknoll, N.Y.: Orbis Press, 1973.

Hanson, Paul D. *The People Called: The Growth of Community in the Bible.* San Francisco: Harper & Row, 1986.

Hasbany, Richard, ed. *Homosexuality and Religion.* Binghamton, N.Y.: Harrington Park Press, 1989.

Helminiak, Daniel. *What the Bible Really Says about Homosexuality.* San Francisco: Alamo Square Press, 1994.

Heyward, Carter. "Coming Out and Relational Empowerment: A Lesbian Feminist Theological Perspective." Stone Center Colloquium Series, Episcopal Divinity School, Cambridge, Mass., 1989.

———. *Our Passion for Justice: Images of Power, Sexuality, and Liberation.* New York: The Pilgrim Press, 1984.

————. *Speaking of Christ: A Lesbian Feminist Voice.* New York: The Pilgrim Press, 1989.

————. *Touching Our Strength: The Erotic as Power and the Love of God.* New York: Harper & Row, 1989.

Katz, Jonathan. *Gay American History: Lesbians and Gay Men in the U.S.A.* New York: Meridian Books, 1992.

Luepnitz, Deborah Anna. *The Family Interpreted: Feminist Theory in Clinical Practice.* New York: Basic Books, 1988.

Marcellino, Elizabeth Mary. "Relationships among Internalized Homonegativity, Self-Concept, and Images of God in Gay and Lesbian Individuals." Ph.D. diss., Boston University, 1995.

Margolies, Liz, Martha Becker, and Karla Jackson-Brewer. "Internalized Homophobia: Identifying and Treating the Oppressor Within." In *Lesbian Psychologies: Explorations and Challenges,* edited by Boston Lesbian Psychologies Collective. Urbana and Chicago: University of Illinois Press, 1987.

McNeill, John J. *Taking a Chance on God: Liberating Theology for Gays, Lesbians, and Their Lovers, Families, and Friends.* Boston: Beacon Press, 1988.

Metzger, Bruce M., and Roland E. Murphy, eds. *The New Oxford Annotated Bible, New Revised Version.* New York: Oxford University Press, 1991.

Minuchin, Salvador. *Families and Family Therapy.* Cambridge: Harvard University Press, 1974.

Morrison, Melanie. *The Grace of Coming Home: Spirituality, Sexuality, and the Struggle for Justice.* Cleveland: The Pilgrim Press, 1995.

Morton, Nelle. *The Journey Is Home.* Boston: Beacon Press, 1985.

Nelson, James B. *Embodiment: An Approach to Sexuality and Christian Theology.* Minneapolis: Augsburg Press, 1978.

Nichols, Michael. *Family Therapy: Concepts and Methods.* Boston: Allyn & Bacon, 1984.

Niebuhr, Reinhold. *Leaves from the Notebook of a Tamed Cynic.* Chicago: Willett, Clark, & Colby, 1929.

"ONA Report, The." Ann B. Day, editor. Holden, Mass.: United Church Coalition for Lesbian/Gay Concerns, 1995.

O'Neill, Craig, and Kathleen Ritter. *Coming Out Within: Stages of Spiritual Awakening for Lesbians and Gay Men, the Journey from Loss to Transformation.* New York: HarperCollins, 1992.

Pharr, Suzanne. *Homophobia: A Weapon of Sexism.* Little Rock: Chardon Press, 1988.

Presbyterian Church, USA, General Assembly Special Committee on Human Sexuality. "Keeping Body and Soul Together: Sexuality, Spirituality, and Social Justice." *Reports to the 203rd General Assembly,* 1991.

Reconciling Congregation Program. "Welcoming Churches: A Growing Ecumenical Movement." *Open Hands: Resources of Ministries Affirming the Diversity of Human Sexuality* 8, no. 3 (winter 1993).

Rose, Suzanna. "Sexual Pride and Shame in Lesbians." In *Lesbian and Gay Psychology: Theory, Practice, and Clinical Applications,* edited by Beverly Greene and Gregory M. Herek. Thousand Oaks, Calif.: Sage Publications, 1994.

Russell, Letty M. *Church in the Round: Feminist Interpretation of the Church.* Louisville, Ky.: Westminster John Knox Press, 1993.

Scanzoni, Letha, and Virginia Ramey Mollenkott. *Is the Homosexual My Neighbor? A Positive Christian Response.* Rev. ed. San Francisco: HarperSanFrancisco, 1994.

Segundo, Juan Luis. *The Liberation of Theology.* Maryknoll, N.Y.: Orbis Press, 1976.

Silverstein, Charles, ed. *Gays, Lesbians, and Their Therapists: Studies in Psychotherapy.* New York: W. W. Norton, 1991.

Tabb, William K. *Churches in Struggle: Liberation Theologies and Social Change in America.* New York: William K. Tabb, 1986.

United Church Coalition for Lesbian/Gay Concerns. "Open and Affirming Churches in the UCC: Update '93, a Report from Sixty-Four ONA Congregations about Studying, Declaring, and Living an Open and Affirming Commitment." Holden, Mass.: United Church Coalition, 1993.

Vaid, Irvashi. *Virtual Equality: The Mainstreaming of Gay and Lesbian Liberation.* New York: Anchor books, 1995.

Webber, George W. *Today's Church: A Community of Exiles and Pilgrims.* Nashville: Abingdon Press, 1979.

Weinberg, George. *Society and the Healthy Homosexual.* New York: St. Martin's Press, 1972.

White, Mel. *Stranger at the Gate: To Be Gay and Christian in America.* New York: Penguin Books, 1994.

Williams, Robert. *Just as I Am: A Practical Guide to Being Out, Proud, and Christian.* New York: Crown Publishers, 1992.